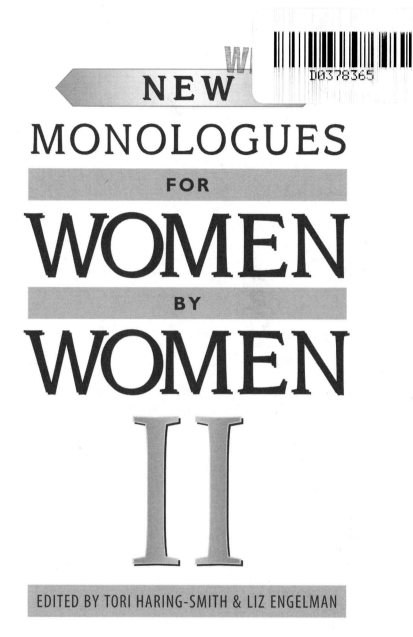

NEW
MONOLOGUES
FOR
WOMEN
BY
WOMEN
II

EDITED BY TORI HARING-SMITH & LIZ ENGELMAN

HEINEMANN
Portsmouth, NH

D0378365

Heinemann
A division of Reed Elsevier Inc.
361 Hanover Street
Portsmouth, NH 03801–3912
www.heinemanndrama.com

Offices and agents throughout the world

Performance rights material can be found on page 157.

Library of Congress Cataloging-in-Publication Data
New monologues for women by women / edited by Tori Haring-Smith and Liz Engelman.
    p. cm.
Includes index.
ISBN 0-325-00626-1 (Vol. I) (alk. paper)
ISBN 0-325-00718-7 (Vol. II)
    1. Monologues. 2. Acting—Auditions. 3. American drama—20th century. 4. Women—Drama. I. Haring-Smith, Tori. II. Engelman, Liz.
PN2080.N49 2004
808.82'45'080082—dc22   2004001419

Editor: Lisa A. Barnett
Production: Elizabeth Valway
Typesetter: Argosy
Cover design: Jenny Jensen Greenleaf
Manufacturing: Jamie Carter

Printed in the United States of America on acid-free paper
09 08 07 06 05 VP 1 2 3 4 5

Contents

Subject Index

Politics

Religion

Sex and Desire

Violence and Revenge

Olesker, Verdure
Rapi, Tricky

Most of the monologues in this collection can be performed by actors of any age, but the following are particularly well suited for younger or more senior women by virtue of their subject matter, situation, or language.

Monologues Particularly Suited for Actors 20 or Younger

Alexander, Pralaya
Appleby, Fritz Perls Is My (tor)Mentor
Bustamante, Set Up
Hagan, My Mother
Harrington, Excerpt from *Marathon Dancing*
Rice, Song of My Sister
Tuan, Excerpt form *Ajax (por nobody)*
Walat, Excerpt from *Rotten State*

Monologues Particularly Suited for Actors Older than 60

Dillman, Years Ago
Franks, Hay
Hudes, *Ingerto* (Plant Fusion)
Hunter, Mrs. Pugh
Thomas, The Gamester
Wiechmann, Widow's Walk

Introduction

London. Paris. New Zealand. Vancouver. Miami. San Francisco. Austin. Look like the cities on a Tiffany's window, but they're not. They are only a sampling of the cities where women writers have had their words spoken and heard. This volume of monologues by women features artists from coast to coast, continent to continent—and will especially make you want to spend a good deal of time in Texas, from where many of these voices seem to hail.

Not only do these writers come from everywhere, they come at writing from every angle. As you read through this volume, pay as much attention to the biographies of the writers as to their words. Their bios prove that one can hold many jobs in life, have a variety of occupations and hobbies, and still be a writer. Take monologist Molly Rice, for example, who has alternately been a rock musician, a fry cook, a professional trainer, a cancer information specialist, and a hotel lounge promoter. Or Freyda Thomas, who not only translates and adapts Molière and Regnard, but has also been a cruiseship chanteuse (entertaining audiences from New York to Bora Bora), a high school French teacher, a banjo bandleader, a realtor, an office manager, a dog walker, and a nanny. What better training is there for a writer? Or, for that matter, for an actor? We can think of none. Women wearing the hats of short-story writers, performers, novelists, educators, producers, journalists, screenwriters, and visual artists have contributed their words, humor, pain, and passions to this volume. Expressing these words on the page isn't necessarily easy, but these women prove that it is possible.

Now *you* have the chance to express their words, passions, and pain on the stage, which is equally difficult, and equally possible. Not everyone is an actor, but many people can act. And here's your chance. If you aren't tempted yet, how's this:

Skim through this volume and you will find delicious experiences with: husbands-to-be, husbands disappeared, and the ex-husband in trailer #6. Revenge fantasies of a not-so-happy Happy Housekeeper. Sex fantasies with none other than the pizza guy. Shopping for shoes. Women missing men. Women wanting men. Women giving men up. Women not giving a hoot. Daughters with fathers, daughters without. Who do you want to be? And if your appetite isn't whetted yet, read on and find out why hay is an emotional crop, why special gifts often cause the biggest problems, and what thoughts just one wasp can inspire. And, of course, ponder the joys of water ballet. . . . There is something here for everyone. What's in it for you?

As these writers illustrate, stories come from all walks of life. They come out of the least expected places, as well as the obvious. Big ideas grow out of little moments, and small revelations emerge from big events. Everyone has a story to tell, something to express, something they feel. Tiffany's window or not, these gems are indeed forever. They are universal in their specificity, they shine in your hands. They live on through you, because through you, they get told. The monologues collected in this edition are the best of the best. And there are more to come. Perform one now, write one later. Hopefully, it's for the next volume!!

—Liz Engelman, Tori Haring-Smith

Tips on Auditioning with a Monologue

Choosing a Monologue

In order to perform a monologue well, you should have some personal connection to it. You need to understand the character's emotion, and be passionate about her concerns. After all, you are going to have to explore this character in depth and then generate enough energy to make her live for your audience. In some cases, actors are drawn to monologue characters because they have undergone similar experiences. If the character is talking about death, and you have recently lost a loved one, you may be able to share something of yourself—your grief—through bringing the character to life. Remember, acting is about sharing yourself. That's one reason why actors must learn to be vulnerable and to relax. When you audition, your audience wants to know who you are, as well as who you can be. Your choice of a monologue often reveals you, so choose carefully.

It is common advice that monologues should talk about the present, not just recount memories from the past. I think this advice, while well-intentioned, is artificially limiting. There is nothing wrong with a monologue that tells a story from the past as long as you, the actor, make it present and active. As long as the story is a vital part of the character you develop, it will stir emotions, shape interactions, and reveal layers within the character. Remember that all monologues have at least one silent stage partner, someone who is listening and responding to the character, perhaps driving the character to keep speaking. Sometimes the silent partner is another character, sometimes another facet of the speaker, and sometimes the theatre audience. As long as the monologue connects with your passions, you will be able to make it live for your silent stage partner and for your audience.

Even though a monologue springs from the interaction of two characters, it must not be too dependent on the context of the play if it is going to stand on its own in an audition. That is, the monologue needs to make sense and be important in its own right—not because of its function within the play as a whole. Many of the most exciting monologues in full-length plays simply cannot stand on their own, because in isolation they do not reveal the character fully enough. Most successful audition monologues do not refer to too many people other than the speaker. It's difficult to keep track of a woman's lover, husband, daughter, and business associate all in one two-minute monologue! The primary purpose of a monologue is to show-case you, not the play or the playwright. If a monologue is well-chosen, it should not require any introduction beyond the title of the play.

It is important that a monologue (or a pair of monologues, if you are performing two together) allows you to show a range of emotional, physical, and vocal qualities. While you can create range by choosing a pair of contrasting monologues, each piece you do should have variety within it. The emotional state of the character needs to be dynamic, so that you can show more than one side of your emotional, physical, and vocal life. If you are choosing a pair of monologues, you will probably want to find speeches on different subjects with differing tones.

When choosing a monologue, you should try to find material that will be new to your audience. When I audition large numbers of people, I hear the same monologues over and again. Sometimes I can't even force myself to listen to painfully familiar pieces like the twirler from *In the Boom-Boom Room*. When you choose a classical monologue, think about how many Juliets or Kates your auditioners will have heard on the professional stage and in auditions. Try to find some new material. Women playwrights from the medieval, Renaissance, Restoration, and eighteenth century are just now being redis-covered and published. Look for collections of their work, and you may find wonderful new monologues. Although this collection will not help you find a classical monologue, it will provide you with more than fifty previously unpublished or very hard-to-find contemporary pieces.

Be sure that the monologue is suitable for you as well as for the theatre or film for which you are auditioning. This does not mean that the character needs to match you identically in race, gender, age, or geographical location. Just be sure that you understand the character and how she responds to life. If you feel that you would respond as she does, you probably have a sympathetic relationship to the character. If you are playing someone much older or younger than yourself, do not "play age"—play yourself. Also avoid pieces that require a strong accent, unless you are told that you need to demonstrate particular dialect abilities. Some people have an accented piece in their storehouse of "extra" monologues—those that are not their primary audition pieces but are available if auditioners want to see more.

Think about the suitability of your monologue for the medium in which you are auditioning. If you are being seen for television work, the monologue should be rated PG. If you have been called for a particular role, try to find a monologue that is generally linked to that script or role (i.e., use a comic piece if you're auditioning for a comedy), but is not from the script itself. The auditioners will have all kinds of preconceived notions about the roles they are casting. If you pull a monologue from the play they have been dreaming about for several months, you may not seem right to them if your interpretation of the character does not match their ideal for it. If the auditioners want to see you in the part, they will ask for a cold reading.

Finally, think about the length of your monologues. Do not cram so much into your two or three minutes that you feel rushed while you are performing. Respect the time limits set by the auditioners. Some of the monologues in this book are obviously too long to be done in an audition, and you will have to cut them. But having access to the entire monologue gives you a fuller sense of context and offers you material for longer performances in showcases and workshops.

Preparing and Rehearsing

As you rehearse your monologue, either alone or with a coach, use the techniques that have been most successful for you in preparing full-length roles. If the piece is from a longer work, read that play. Do not rely on the longer work to "explain" the character—after all, your auditioners may not know the piece. The monologue must stand on its own as a comprehensible piece, telling the auditioners all they need to know about your character. Also, don't let the full play's context limit you. Don't assume that because the character in the play is insane, your interpretation must also reveal insanity.

More important than any research in the library, more important even than reading the full script is careful examination of the specific text that you are going to present. Think about the character drawn there and ask yourself the usual character-development questions, including:

- Who is this person talking to? Does that shift at any point during the piece? What does the listener want from the speaker?
- What question or event is the speaker responding to? What happened just before she began to speak?
- What does the speaker need? Why does she keep on speaking? (Make this need as important as possible.)
- What are the conflicts within the speaker and between the speaker and her listener(s)?
- What does the speaker's language reveal about her? What is the speaker's favorite word in this monologue?
- How is the speaker different after she has said her piece than before? What has she gained, lost, or discovered?
- What line in the monologue is the most important? Where does the speech make emotional turns? Where does it reach a climax?

As you explore the character, keep reassuring yourself that you are not necessarily looking for the "right" answers to your character questions. You are looking for emotionally truthful answers that you can play. Be faithful to your own experience and your own sense of truth—not to what someone else thinks that the character should be like. Do not be satisfied with quick, easy answers. Keep probing.

As you work on the character, consider her vocal and physical life. Would she sit down, or is she too overwrought? Does she try to hide her strong emotions behind civilized, controlled speech, or does she speak out? Experiment with different business you might give the character as well. Is she knitting while she talks? Is she fidgeting with a button? Putting on make-up? Consider her body stance. Does she stand tall? Hunch forward? Sit primly? Be sure that you make choices that allow you to keep your head up and that do not force you to move so frenetically that the auditioners cannot see you from the movement. Know where your silent partner is. Do not make the auditioner a silent partner—no one wants to be forced to participate in an actor's piece. Does the silent partner move at any point? If so, ask yourself where, when, and how?

As you rehearse, concentrate on your primary goal of making the character present and active. Command attention—think of what Linda Loman says about Willy—"Attention must be paid." If you know what the character wants, then you will have no trouble bringing that need out for the audience.

Once you begin to put your actual performance together, consider how you will start. Your introduction and your piece are part of the performance, because you are in fact "on" from the moment that you walk through the doors of the audition room or onto the stage. Practice introducing yourself pleasantly and efficiently:

> Hello. My name is _____, and today I'll be doing monologues from Julie Jensen's *Water Lilies* and Sarah Ruhl's *The Clean House*.

Then work on the transition into your first monologue. Take a moment to visualize your character's situation, to ground yourself in her needs, to place your silent partner, and to think about the question or event that you are responding to. Practice this kind of preparation, and you will not need more than five to ten seconds to accomplish it.

Work through the transitions between monologues in the same way. After you have chosen an order for your pieces, consider how you will move smoothly from one to the other. Be sure that you complete the first monologue, give it a beat to sink in, then alter your physicality in some way, and quickly launch into the second piece. As you rehearse, have someone time your work. Be sure that you are well within the time limits set by the audition. When you are performing, you want to be able to think about the character, not the clock. Take your time to live the character fully but not self-indulgently. And, above all, don't be afraid of being boring. If you think you're boring, you're going to telegraph that to your auditioners, and your worst nightmare will come true.

Plan what you are going to wear to the audition. Think of something that complements your body type and doesn't distort your presentation of either of your characters. You do not want to look costumed during your audition; you want to look as much like yourself as you can. The goal of the audition is to reveal yourself and the range of your abilities. You may want to costume one character by adding or taking off a jacket or scarf, but do not plan elaborate costume changes. Most people do not change costume at all during their auditions. After all, you should be able to present the character without relying on a costume to support you. Similarly, you may need one small prop in one of your monologues—a pencil, a book. If you need more props than that, you have not chosen an appropriate audition piece. Remember that the only furniture you can count on having is a folding metal chair. Try to be as self-sufficient as possible, and not to rely on costumes, props, or furniture. Your acting—not the technical aspects of your performance—must be the focus. Your auditioners should remember you, not your costume.

As you rehearse, keep exploring. Take risks—that's what rehearsals are for. If you find that you are afraid of looking foolish—playing either too big or too small—face your fears. Do the monologue as you fear it might be seen at its very worst. Facing your fears helps them dissolve away. But if you don't face them, enact them, and experience your worst nightmare in the safety of a rehearsal, your fears will limit your spontaneity and make you censor yourself. Sometimes, you will discover that your worst nightmare may have been an excellent choice for the piece—you were just afraid of taking the chance. Don't be afraid to be quirky or bold.

Some people hire coaches to help them prepare monologue work. Whether you rehearse alone or with a coach, at some point you need to practice performing your work in front of different audiences. Don't always practice or perform in the same studio. Move around. Get used to performing anywhere, so that the strangeness of the audition situation will not throw you. If you can perform with equal concentration and comfort in a living room, on a stage, in a classroom, and out of doors, you're probably well prepared for your audition.

Presenting Yourself and Your Work

Before your audition, try not to establish expectations. Of course, you should be aware of any rules that have been set for the audition—number and type of pieces you should present, time limits—but don't establish expectations for the audition process itself. Don't try to visualize the room because you may be surprised and have to deal with that surprise when you should be acting. If you think, "Oh, I'll be up on a big stage in a 2,000-seat auditorium," and you end up auditioning in a hotel conference room, you'll have trouble making immediate adjustments, and doing so will distract you from concentrating on the monologue.

Don't even make assumptions about the behavior or the number of the people who will be watching you. Sometimes you will be performing for one person, sometimes for fifty or sixty in combined auditions such as Strawhat or Midwest Theatre Auditions. Don't anticipate rapt attention from your auditors. They may look at you intently, they may eat while you perform (they often don't get lunch breaks), or they may pass papers around or talk about you. Don't be surprised, don't be thrown. Just do your work and let them do theirs. It is hard not to be offended if someone is talking while you perform, but keep your concentration on your own work. Remember, they may be saying, "She's perfect for the part, isn't she?"

Get a good night's sleep before your audition and wear comfortable clothes. If you're going on a callback, wear the same or similar clothes that you wore to the first audition. If the auditioners liked that person, they will both remember and like a similar looking one during callbacks. Wearing a T-shirt and jeans to an initial audition and then a suit to the callbacks only confuses the people who are trying to find the real you. Bring extra copies of your picture and resume in case you need them.

Know where you are going and give yourself plenty of time to get there. You don't want to be nervous about your punctuality. There may be forms to fill out, and you will want to warm up before you audition. Find a quiet space to center yourself, warm up vocally and physically, and run over your piece to be sure that you are comfortable with it. If you can't find a private space, just close your eyes, focus, and take yourself through the piece in your head. Follow the emotional track of the character and visualize your silent partner. In other words, perform in your head. This is the same practice that professional athletes engage in when they visualize themselves making a free-throw or kicking a goal before they act.

When it is time for you to audition, you will be admitted into the audition room by a monitor or the casting director. In most cases, you or the casting director will have sent your picture and resume to the director. If that is not the case, hand the picture and resume to the director as you enter the room and cross to the audition area. If the director initiates a conversation, respond politely and efficiently. Think of this as a cocktail conversation. Most directors, though, will not initiate conversation. They're rushed, and they just want to see who you are.

As soon as you enter the room, seize the space. Walk confidently and know that for the next three minutes, you are in charge of what happens in that space. It is all too easy to experience auditions as a kind of meat market, in which you are just a number. In fact, auditions are often like this, but you must never present yourself as "just one more actor." Take the stage. Know that you're important.

If you need to move a chair or set up the space, do so quickly. Then pause to be sure that the director is ready for you to proceed. In some cases, a monitor will indicate when you should begin. Introduce yourself and your piece, making eye contact with the director or with as many of a large group of directors as possible. This is the only time during the formal part of the audition that you should make direct eye contact with the auditioners. Set up your space so that you are facing the auditioners, but put your silent partner to one side of them or just behind them. Once your introduction is over, take a few seconds (no more) to focus completely on your work and then go.

At the end of the performance, wait a beat, break character, and then say, "Thank you." If, for some reason, the director wants to see more of you, you may be asked to do a cold reading or additional monologues. Always have some additional work in reserve. It is not uncommon, especially in graduate school auditions, for directors to request specific types of monologues. "Do you have something more upbeat?" "Can you show us a more vulnerable character?" "Do you have something in verse?" You can never be prepared for all requests, but have a supply of work at your beck and call. If you are not asked to do additional work, however, don't be depressed. You may not have suited the role, or you may have been so perfect that the auditioners know immediately that they want to see you at callbacks.

When you've finished, never comment on your own work—especially to apologize. The most important thing is to be confident and to look like you're having a good time throughout the ordeal. Don't comment on your own work by scowling, frowning, or shrugging as you walk away.

Once you have left the audition, try not to second-guess the director. Even if the director seemed to respond well to your work, don't begin to fantasize about what it will be like to work with that director or on that project. If you don't get the part, you'll just be doubly disappointed. Every actor needs a strong support system. You put yourself on the line daily—you are the product that you are selling—and although you may know that not everyone wants or needs your product, it is never easy to take rejection. Remember that even famous actors face rejection every day. Keeping faith in yourself and in those around you who stay by you in your times of need will see you through and keep you sane.

Auditioning is an actor's job. It can be a nightmare, but it can also be fun. You meet lots of different people, get tips on upcoming projects, and have a chance, however brief, to perform. Just keep reminding yourself that you are in control of your performance. No matter how good you are, you will only be right for some roles. Can you imagine Roseanne Arnold as a sensitive figure skater? Keep true to your own sense of self, keep polishing your acting skills, and be sure that you have other ways of measuring your self-worth aside from getting cast in any one given role.

—Tori Haring-Smith

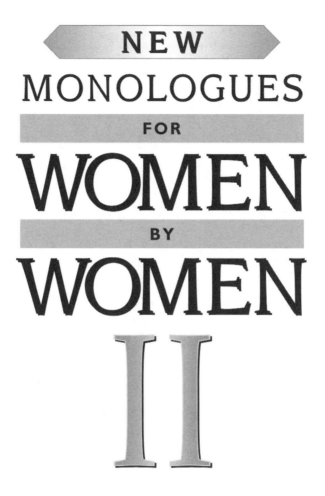

NEW
MONOLOGUES
FOR
WOMEN
BY
WOMEN
II

Pralaya

ZAKIYYAH ALEXANDER

CALICO, a fifteen-year-old girl living in New York City who turns tricks and cuts herself for pleasure, reminisces about love and innocence lost.

CALICO: Where is this fucking love shit I hear all the time? Fucking blasting on the radio, in the movies, on a t-shirt love type shit? This dude was pretty fucking cool, right? Fucking cool as hell. We were like soul mates and shit, fucking nickel and diming together. Holding hands and shit like some kind a wack ass teen romance, right? He was giving me his clothes to wear, y'know? Scribbling down poetry on napkins from diners. And when we kissed. He tasted of strawberry sherbet, mixed with Lucky Strikes, mixed with this heavy that was so deep it went up your nose, right, like you felt it in every fucking part of your body. Dude got me wet just smelling his smell. Made me weak in the knees. And things were so cool I didn't even believe this was my life, right? Cuz we were kissing in the rain, laughing and shit cuz life was this beautiful thing, it was actually ours to enjoy. And I was all, fuck, man, I'm happy. Who knew you could actually for real be happy?

Then one day he was gone. Not a word. No good-bye, have a nice life type shit. Just gone. Ghost. Disappeared. Suddenly I was really alone. And I was like, fuck, this is what alone is. Alone is so much worse after you have known what we is.

Love is not used in fucking. Now I fuck when I have to. A necessary evil. Doesn't matter. There is nothing left to make this shit real. If I erased myself—no one would know. I am lost.

Excerpt from *It Doesn't Take a Tornado*

ROSANNA YAMAGIWA ALFARO

A woman sits in front of her trailer talking to a TV reporter and her camera crew. Wreckage everywhere, but the woman's trailer is intact.

Do I have a minute to spare? Young lady, you can have a minute, an hour . . . you can have the rest of my life, if you want it. I've already talked to the Fire Chief—he's a nice man—and the Deputy Coroner—who's a real jerk—and someone from the County Sheriff's Office. Well, I guess I'm the only one left around here to talk to. Everyone else is lying in the morgue or, worse yet, the city hospital. It was awful. My dog, Hank? I saw him sailing through the air, all seventy pounds of him. He just flew past along with the two cats. Damn.

　　The trailer's OK. Thank God. The forest behind me—untouched. Not a branch, not a twig fell to the ground. You don't believe me? Go look for yourself. Tornadoes are attracted to metal—that's why my trailer's out of the loop, backed up against the forest. I was in my bathtub with a mattress over my head, but all the time I felt I'd come out of this just fine—which I did, thank God.

　　Most everyone else, they lost all they had. Howie and Janice in No. 2? They were headed for a divorce, and this will speed things up, you betcha. That shiny sixty-five-foot trailer that was trucked in here just yesterday? When its owners come looking for it, they'll find it on its side over there in the swamp. I sat out here and watched the whole thing until it got too close. I tell, you, it was amazing. The smell of the electricity in the air, the way that funnel touched down here, then there, taking our power lines, boom! Kaboom! Then it sat right down on the trailer park and wiped it off the face of the earth.

It's a sad business. My ex-husband in No. 6? Roof fell in on top of him and broke his back. (*Beat*) Oh, don't be too sorry. I'm certainly not. Put him out of his misery, poor slob. (*Beat*) Children? Two of them. Molly's in California. Matt, in Florida, I think. I tell you, it doesn't take a high wind to scatter a family to the four corners of the earth. It doesn't take a killer tornado. Other accidents can throw you off course. (*Beat*)

The day I kicked him out of my house it was like I was ridding myself of this huge weight that was killing me. I took everything of his I could find and threw it out after him—his six packs, his stacks of *Hustler*, his armchair. I tell you it was like throwing boulders, uprooting trees, and hurling them at him. Well, now it seems God's seen fit to finish up my work. It takes a tornado to clean house.

The Order of Things

JANET ALLARD

JUDY sits at a table. She holds a purse.

JUDY: I know there is a certain way the world should work. A certain order to things, a certain way it spins, certain rules like gravity, a certain way that water flows, waterfalls fall, rivers only flow one way. I think. Tides. These things are governed by laws that we can't see. I know this. But why is it with people—Are you listening honey? Why is it with people that the only ones who get somewhere in this world are those who are willing to go against the flow, to carve out their own way in the rock. To become your own river, traveling by your own rules. Do you see what I'm saying? You love me for that, I know you love me for the way I don't fit into the world, to my place in the world, that I'm a square peg who doesn't even try to fit into the round whole, because WHY? I know you love me because I upset the order of things, I create my own rules. I don't wait for anyone to tell me who I can be or who I am or what I can do, I never walk on the path I bushwhack my own path, Jim, I carve my own course for my life. Because, can you put down your fork for a second, see Jim. You love me, right? You love me, right, I know that and I'm certain of that and even more than that, no, no more wine, thank you. Even more than that, I'm certain that you love me for who I am. Because you know me, and you know I am a woman who goes against the laws of gravity, who goes against the ebb and flow of tides, who carves out her own way, so the question is, why should I wait for you to . . . I mean, I'm going out on a limb here, I'm risking something here, to do something here. I mean this might upset you at first. You might have an unfavorable reaction to this at first, but I want you to ask yourself are you in love with a woman who ACTS or a

4

woman who WAITS. Do you believe there will be a woman president? Soon? Of course, okay, a little more wine, of course. Of course there will be, and that will be a huge step for our country, but it won't topple the order of the world, the unspoken order of the world where I have to wait and wait and wait for you to . . .

Jim, I love you, do you love me? I know you do. Then this should come as no surprise. (*She rifles through her purse.*) Then it should not be a surprise to you that I, that we, that, don't you think it's time (it was in here, hold on—) I mean I've waited for some time, I've tried to hold back here, to let the natural order of things take its course, to allow you to, but then I thought, why? What's the real crime in this, what's the real crime of asking you the question I need to ask you that I'm dying to ask you, of taking things in my own hands and then I think but what will my mother say, what will the neighbors say, will you be discontent and emasculated and will I wonder forever if you really loved me, because I didn't let you catch me like a small prey, like I hunted you instead of you hunting me, that if I pursue you instead of you pursuing me, and my mother would say if he wanted to, he'd ASK you, but . . . (*She empties her purse out on the table.*) Don't you think it's time that. . . . Things just get lost in here, they just disappear, talk about chaos, talk about upsetting the order of things, the world is not a civilized place! The order we perceive is PERCEIVED it's as see-through as a dream. There's CHAOS everywhere. (*She holds up a ring box.*) Oh.

What I wanted to ask you Jim, what I want to say—

I know this upsets the usual order of things, but (where's the crime in that and) Jim?

Will you?

Marry me?

Shuttle to Houston

JANET ALLARD

A WOMAN *in a space suit.*

WOMAN: Shuttle to Houston, shuttle to Houston. Time is passing and I'm traveling farther and farther into—It's beautiful. Space. It's gorgeous, falling away from . . .

Shuttle to Houston, shuttle to Houston, you'd be amazed by what you can see from this distance, the perspective, Houston, I'm traveling, traveling fast toward what's beautiful.

Shuttle to Houston, shuttle to Houston you look like a big glowing sphere from here, do you copy. Do you copy? Houston? I haven't missed home, missed home base Houston, as much as I thought. Houston? Hello? I thought I'd miss you more, Houston. Do you think it's because I've been distracted by all this beauty out here and my world seems to be cracking open and I'm seeing the world as I've never seen it, do you think Houston that maybe I haven't missed—I'm traveling Houston, farther and farther into, it's beautiful, space, it's gorgeous.

Shuttle to Houston, shuttle to Houston, do you copy. Come in Houston? Roger? Houston? Roger? Are you there?

I know I'm supposed to prepare for re-entry, Houston, but I'm afraid, I'm afraid. Shuttle to Houston, I'm afraid that's not possible. Roger? You are beautiful from here, do you copy, shuttle to shuttle to, I've got a light here, I've got an uh-oh, light, "check engine" light on here, Houston, do you copy, the light is on and blinking on and blinking red blinking red, Houston? I've got a sound here, I've got a strange sound Houston, a rattling coming apart sound and I can't tell where it's coming from, shuttle to Houston, can you hear me, life's not the same without you, but I'm breaking open, I'm traveling faster and faster and closer and closer to what's real, what's beautiful and I want to take you with me, but Roger, I'm coming apart. Shuttle to Houston, can anyone tell me what that sound is? I'm shaking Houston, I'm shaking. I'm making that sound. I think that sound, that coming apart sound is coming from me.

Hello? Can anyone hear me? Roger? I'm not coming back.

Shuttle to Houston, you've always told me to follow my dreams, Houston, to dream big and go there and Houston you were right, you are right Houston, here I am, breaking outside of my little world. I'm stepping out of the shuttle Houston, I'm stepping out, roger dodger, do you copy, if we lose the connection for a minute don't be alarmed, all will be well, I'm stepping out of the shuttle now, out into blind space, wide open here I go one foot—

Shuttle to Houston, shuttle to Houston, this is magnificent. There's nothing Houston. Nothing out here but my voice. But me. Roger. And I'm weightless. Do you copy, weightless.

I know you need me. But I'm not coming back, over, do you copy over, do you read me over, do you know what I'm saying do you hear me over and over, over, I'm losing the connection Roger, over do you know, over, do you know what I'm saying, over, do you copy over do you read over do you know who I am, I'm traveling Roger, at a million miles per second the universe is falling away, I can no longer see our house, or the planet I belong to, I'm out here now over over over do you copy over. Over. I. Over. You, over, over over over over over

Out.

Fritz Perls Is My (tor)Mentor

ELIZABETH APPLEBY

LIZ: It's Wednesday, eight years ago. My father's in the final stages of cancer. I call home and my mother answers: "I have great news, Liz. Dad's dead! Can't talk now, I'm on the line with the undertaker." That's how she sounded, like she was dating! "No time, dear. I'm *making plans* with the undertaker." I'm stunned. But I'm also relieved. My father suffered for ten years. And my mother was with him for every moment of that suffering. Maybe *that's* what this is: "No time, dear," maybe my mother's just letting go.

I call her the next day, Thursday. She tells me she just visited the funeral home . . . spent time with Dad. "Mom, you spent time with Dad? Where do they keep him?" "In the freezer, dear. They took him out. I sat with him. You know, he's so much more present now than he was before." And I ask her if it didn't feel strange and she says: "Well you know Dad had so little time for me. Now I can finally enjoy him."

And I *know* what she's talking about: My father was a man who held office hours in order to say I love you. She once called him an emotional refrigerator . . . but he's thawed so much during his illness. . . .

The Funeral is for Sunday. I call home. My mother tells me she's been visiting again. Says she's "kissed his hands and feet." Wait, she's *touched* my father? But he was so untouchable in life. And I don't know which is more alarming . . . the fear that I won't be *able* to, won't be *brave* enough to touch my dead father, or my envy that my mother already has, has touched him, and that somehow she's now closer to him. . . . I mean I know she's his *wife*, but I always hoped *I* was closer to him.

And then my mother tells me she and my sister Sarah are going one last time to the funeral home. And this changes everything. Sarah's going?! And suddenly this is no longer about my father or that he's dead or that I even love him. No, now I've gotta touch him, I've gotta touch him longer than Sarah does.

The Love Shopper

HEIDI ARNESON

Wanna know the truth? . . . I don't like to shop. I come from farm stock. They went through the Great Depression. Saved the water in the sink. Cut the buttons off the old clothes to sew onto the new ones. Sewed the feed sacks into Sunday frocks, made the torn socks into throw rugs, fed the kitchen scraps to the barn cats, wove the bread bags into fruit bowls, an' the heart bone connected to the hip bone, hip bone connected to the chair seat, an', if the chair leg was too tall, you sawed it off to fit you, an' you lived in a beautiful kingdom where you shaped the world to your unique needs, one-of-a-kind, with your work-brown hands, an' not a thing was wasted. Honey, if you don't have it, you can damn well figure out a way to make it. Course, you can't do that with everything nowadays—how the hell am I gonna throw together a Microtec 4900 scanner from kitchen scraps?

So I need a new sole for my shoes? Where do I go? Len's Riverside Amaco! "Len, you got an old tire for me?" "Help yourself, baby. We got 23 back of the building." I walk on Firestones some stranger drove across America. I got all this surplus love.

So I'm standing at the clothes rack at Saver's. An' I got my hands on a red dress, an' I got my shopping blinders on, to block out the reality of all the beating human hearts around me. An' behind me is a family talking an' shopping in Spanish: "*Quando quando pero pero*," I don't sprechen-zee Espanol, but I know what I want, an' I don't want this dress. . . . I want to turn around and look in the eyes of the woman. Turn around and look in the eyes of the man. Turn around an' look in the eyes of the child. What do we do when we shop? Look at objects. Touch objects. Compare objects. Smell objects. Dream about what we will do with those objects when we get them home.

Cold objects
Put together
On a conveyer belt
By bored strangers
Watchin' the clock
For the time they can go home an' shop shop shop
For cold objects
Put together
On a conveyer belt
By bored strangers
Watchin the clock
For the time they can go home an' shop shop shop

An' it's one-two-three, what are we shoppin' for? Don't ask me, I don't give a damn. You see me at Target, you think I'm shopping? I'm not.

You know the movie *Blue Velvet*? With Isabella Rosellini? Don't matter if you don't. There's a scene in the show where she does something really weird to the hero. We won't go into that now—an' he says, "What are you doing?" An' she smiles an' says, "I'm loving you."

So if you are out shopping at the mall, an' you feel me staring at you all, remember: I don't want to take you home. Don't want to slide you into my hard drive, or smooth you over my shaved thighs. Don't wanna hang you in my closet, screw you in my socket, paint you on my toenails, spray you in my armpit, no. Don't wanna slice an' dice you into bite size pieces. Don't wanna fill you up with gasoline, get inside you, strap myself in, an' drive you through America, no. I just wanna make a connection. So if you are out shopping at the mall, an' you feel me staring at you all, an' you turn around and say, "What the hell are you doing, bitch?" I'll smile and say, "I'm loving you."

The Housekeeper Strikes Back

RACHEL AXLER

PELL, late 20s. She wears an ugly housecleaning uniform.

PELL: It's been a day of reckoning, Astin, and I've discovered something. I am a big loser.

This morning, when the earthquake hit, and the *OED* fell off the shelf and hit you in the head or whatever . . . you know why I didn't get hurt? Because I was already up, Astin. I was up and dressed, in my stupid, ugly brown uniform, cleaning supplies in hand, ready to go out and face my first appointment. And then the house started to roll and tilt, and things began to fall off the walls, and I got a little worried. Not worried about getting hurt, though. Or dying. Or how long I could survive, trapped underground. No—I was worried about Mrs. Knight. Evelyn Knight, my 10:30. I thought about how annoyed she would be when 10:30 came and the cat hairs weren't removed from her couch. Her ugly, beige, fake velvet couch.

And, I mean, the thing is HIDEOUS, Astin. It has these special hypo-allergenic foam cushions, because Mrs. Knight's allergic to her cat, and apparently that helps. How, I don't know. Maybe she breathes through her butt. I swear, though, this cat sheds, like, entire other cats. And every week, I remove the excess cat from the outside of the cushions, hair by hair, until the damn thing is clean. And as I do it, I . . . I fantasize.

Just a minor fantasy, but it keeps me going. . . . Every week, as I clean that couch, I think: if I just took out a tiny bit of the hypo-allergenic foam—just a little each time—and replaced it with cat hair I'd collected from outside the cushion, it'd be, what, only a matter of years, maybe, before the ENTIRE

COUCH was stuffed full of exactly what Mrs. Knight was avoiding! A . . . death couch, effectively! And all because she was too lazy to clean the cat hairs off, herself . . .

Oh my god, I'm evil.

This is what occupies me, Astin! How to hurt the only woman alive who cares that I exist. And actually, that's not even true, is it? I mean, if the earthquake had been worse, and I'd been buried under the rubble, Mrs. Knight would probably wonder where I was briefly, then call the company and hire another Happy Housekeeper. Most likely a Happier Housekeeper. Nobody would care. And I've left no legacy. I'm almost thirty, and I don't even have the guts to begin Project Cat Hair Cushions!

Be glad you got a concussion, Astin. At least you don't have to face how awful we are.

Excerpt from *Dark Boughs Down*

ANNA BAUM

JACKIE, 42, is fantasizing about a police detective who is investigating her husband's disappearance.

JACKIE: I can hear you sweating. I hear you, lying awake. You don't have air conditioning. Or maybe you do, but you don't like to use it; you installed it for your wife. But tonight she's asleep and you're lying there, thinking about me. In the heat. Your pores are open. You're *alive*. I can see it in your eyes. You don't complain because you're a man. But you dream. You dream about a life with a woman who understands you. A woman who accepts her part in this run-down drama called life, but who knows—like you—there's something more.

Your brown, slim stomach rises and falls as you lie on your back, eyes closed. The sheets are damp. There's a million tears in your head, unshed, and your thoughts swim in them, playing like dolphins, like free fish, even though tomorrow they'll be caught on the same damn hooks. But tonight they swim.

You think of me. You let yourself want me. Tomorrow you'll put on your clothes, and your professional demeanor, but tonight you can remember the dress I wore today, the shape it took and the way it moved. The wisp of hair by my ear. The touch of my fingers as I handed you a cup of coffee.

You see I'm trapped and you want to save me. Maybe you'll figure out a way, but for now you lie there thinking of the castle walls, how thick they are, how impossible. And your own wife . . . but there must be a way. There will be a way. Because this feeling, this passion, can't be for nothing.

I can hear you sweating.

Set Up

MONIKA BUSTAMANTE

MOLLY, early 20s, speaks to the audience.

MOLLY (*responding to a flash in the air above her*): Did you see that? A flash like that, it makes me think—sometimes I'm melo-dramatic—but it makes me think that maybe I just had such a big thought, so important, so charged . . . that it surged and cut the power. Briefly. But not just then. Just then I was thinking about donuts.

Dad used to do donuts in the car 'til we were sick. We'd roll all over the place, end up in each other's laps, screaming and laughing. One time my sister peed. She's laughing and peeing, my other sister's screaming, and my dad's trying to watch what's going on in the rearview mirror, still turning the car in furious 360s, he's yelling, "You did what? You did what to my interior?" I was in the front seat. Next to him. Buckled in.

I get dizzy a lot. For no apparent reason. The doctors pon-dered it for years, searched my brain—CATscans, MRIs, the whole bit. No link. No tumors, at least, they didn't think so. Eventually they narrowed it down to my teeth. Said my teeth were too tight. There was mandibular pressure, and if I stood with my jaw locked, teeth clenched, for too long, circulation was interfered with leading to headaches and . . . dizziness. I wore braces for six years to get perfect teeth and these clowns decided they were going to have to reset my jaw to end the problem. Do you know what that means? They literally break your jaw. Break it, and reposition it. I decided to stick with the dizziness. It's great for parties. Makes me the center of attention. One minute I'm serving pretzels and chips, the next, whooo, chex party mix.

The doctors' advice to me, barring the whole skull-cracking business, was to let my mouth hang open. All the time. This was their solution—for me to be a mouthbreather. (*She has a dizzy spell.*) I'm gonna sit.

Did you know that early learning skills, like in preschool children, did you know that the brain process that controls the tongue is linked to motor development? That's why little kids, when they're thinking real hard, they'll have their mouths open, tongues hanging out, they can't help it. Sometimes you catch adults who still do this. You feel sorry for 'em, right, 'cause it's kind of embarrassing to watch. But I do it all the time . . . at home. I think it really helps free up the mind.

Kids like to draw pictures of their parents. I don't remember my mother, but . . . (*Draws a picture on a piece of paper*) this is a picture of my father after he got sick. But most of my life, he looked like—(*Adds a circle to center of the picture*) this. Not a good likeness, but . . . just imagine a man who was the physical embodiment of a hairy ball of dough. (*She adds hair to the donut.*)

My father liked coconut donuts. He used to have to suck his teeth after he ate them 'cause big shreds of it would get caught in between his front teeth. I had the same gap when I was little, but . . . braces. I pulled my braces off myself once. My father had grounded me for something and he took my sisters to the movies. I got the pliers from the garage, locked myself in the bathroom, and presto! I'll never forget what my teeth felt like . . . smooth . . . slimy, even. Clean. Sweet. That was in year four of braces, when I was sixteen. My sister (the one who peed), she came home, took one look at the heap of metal on the floor and screamed. The next day the braces went back on. Dr. Winkey and my father stood behind me discussing my attitude and the progress of my teeth as I was slowly wired back in. They were sure both would straighten out eventually.

I didn't kiss anyone until I was eighteen. I'm not sure if it was because of the braces or not. His name was Richard. He was sixteen and he mowed our grass on the second Sunday of every month for fifteen dollars. He wore green corduroy pants. Always. I pulled up in the driveway and saw him sitting on our front porch drinking one of my dad's beers. I told him I'd tell his parents unless he kissed me. He didn't seem to mind. He smelled like . . . sweat and grass and peanuts and . . . well, beer, I guess. I found plenty of people to kiss after that. Without blackmail.

I have an idea about sex. Aside from any physical pull between two people, aside from being really drunk or really "in love," or whatever, the first time for most people is really just . . . a milestone. A rite of passage. A distinct rebellion. Especially for girls. Good girls don't, right? Who really wants to be a good girl anyway? It's all so hypocritical. Dress me in pink so I look pretty. Dress me in pink so I look innocent. Dress me in pink so I look appealing and sweet, put lots of bows on to untie, lots of ruffles to emphasize, dress me in pink so I look like a good, sweet, untouched, tempting little bundle that never should but definitely, definitely will. If people really wanted to keep their little daughters pure, they'd dress 'em in black—intimidate the hell out of the boys, starting early. Black implies a knowledge of something—teenagers adopt that idea quickly—and knowledge is intimidating to the young. You get older, those ideas change. Black is cool at fourteen. That's when parents should switch to pink.

My father bought me a black dress for the prom. One day he just came home with it, out of nowhere. "Try it on and come show me." I stood in front of my mirror with it on. I looked older. I looked like a wo-man. I showed my father. He blinked, cleared his throat, and nodded. In that order.

What is there in black? It holds nothing and everything. I think it's more frightening for what goes away. I used to be scared of the dark. Literally—click—screaming—click—the lights were back on. One night my father said that there was the earth, right, all bright and sunny. Then along comes an angel to put us all to sleep. And she takes a deep blue scarf and she slowly drags it over the earth. And as soon as it's still, she takes a pin and she pokes little holes through for us to see the light, to remember the sun. And she hangs a lantern to be the moon.

"Daddy," I said. "I'm not afraid of the night. I'm afraid of the dark." I still am.

Prom night. May 23rd, Saturday. I bathed, I showered. I manicured. I pedicured. I concealed, based, powdered mascaraed, and lipsticked. (*Applies lipstick*) Pink. (*Reads label*) "Ready and Waiting." Heels, for the first time in my life. Exactly four months after my first kiss. Getting to be a pro at that. Still haven't had sex, though. Not yet.

I don't know who my date is. I don't know what he looks like. I have been, as they say, set up. The son of one of my father's buddies. My father is a policeman. So is his buddy. His son is nineteen. A freshman in college. He likes to ski. He's in fifteen different clubs. Dad likes the looks of him. We should get along great.

The doorbell rings at eight. Flowers, a kiss on the cheek. "This is my daughter, Molly. Take good care of her." Dad slaps me on my ass . . . what is it? A tag? A punishment? A congratulations? An initiation? I stumble out the door. In the car I get a good look at him. He is tall. He is handsome. He must be getting a new car out of this deal. He doesn't look very happy to be with me. "So," he says. "Where to?" "Dinner?" I say numbly. "Oh, you haven't eaten?" he says. He feigns surprise. "Okay."

We go to a restaurant with plastic tablecloths and paper flowers. I get salad dressing on my dress and tomato sauce in my hair. He doesn't seem to notice. He says almost nothing and yawns periodically. He has beautiful teeth. He does not eat. I pay.

The prom. He sees someone he knows and disappears for twenty minutes. I sit at a table with a girl named Noreen. We smile awkwardly at each other. When he walks back to me, Noreen blinks in disbelief. I take his arm quickly. He takes it back. Then we're on the dance floor and I'm spinning. Around and around and around and I start to laugh and he's laughing too and his teeth are so white and straight and his tuxedo is so black and I am too and I think that I might cry so I just say his name. Gabriel. His name was Gabriel.

And then we're at a party and I had a lot of punch before we got here and a few glasses since and soon I'm friends with everyone in the room and they all like me. And he has his arm around me now and he smells like . . . trees, and his eyes are colored amber and his hair is red. And he kisses me and his tongue is warm and sweet and it fills my mouth and then we're in the closet and I smell cedar and he shuts the door and it's never been so dark. It's never been so dark. And he's taking my dress off, one strap, then the other. I'm cold, and scared, and silly, and I giggle and pull them back. And he takes my shoes off, one foot, then the other. And I'm cold and scared and short and I put them back on. And he's getting mad and he's breathing heavy and suddenly everything the doctors said about gritting teeth and circulation and tension all makes sense and . . . I fainted. I woke up alone. I called his name, fumbled for the door. Cracked it open and caught sight of my legs—hose torn, no shoes. . . it got worse after that.

Nobody was called. No charges were pressed. It was too complicated, Dad said. The circumstances were hazy, he said. I shouldn't have been drinking. I shouldn't have been in the closet. Gabriel was a good boy. I was always too impulsive. Where were the witnesses? Where were the chaperones? I was just lucky I wasn't pregnant. Damn lucky. My sister, the one who peed, she called Dad the gutless wonder—a donut—round, soft, and empty in the middle.

The buddy stopped coming around. Daddy quit the force. We never looked at each other anymore. One day, out of nowhere, he said, "I do the best I can." And I nodded and smiled, the way you do when a child boasts at beating you at checkers.

Daddy got sick after that. And soon he got so sick he would never get well again. Daddy turned yellow cause he was leaking inside, his liver had ruptured. A definite yellow, from the whites of his eyes on down. And then he turned blue, a blue of disuse from the toes on up. The nurses told us he was hanging on. Didn't want to go. Day one his feet were blue. Day two his ankles. "Talk to him," they said. "He can hear you. Tell him it's okay to let go." Day three his shins. "Is he waiting for someone? Tell him to look for the light." Day four his knees. "Have you told him you love him?" I sat by his bed. My chameleon father. Once was fat, now a feather. Translucent. Penetrable. All the relatives had come, all the goodbyes had been said. Day five, his thighs. Day six, his stomach. "Your father must be very strong. Your daddy must love you very much." Day seven, his chest, once a barrel, now concave. (*Kneels by the bed.*) "This can't go on forever, Daddy. The nurses don't know how you do it. They say you're waiting. They say your heart is only supporting an area this big now, just holding on. Are you listening, Daddy? Can you hear me? . . . I forgive you for being quiet."

They put him in a shiny casket and covered it with a flag— a dark blue cloth with the stars already out. The policemen carried him out. There were hundreds there to see it.

Daddy had three girls. He was a policeman. He had crooked teeth. He liked donuts. He had to sit in big chairs. He never smoked. Daddy carried me on his back sometimes. He kept my mother's perfume on his dresser. Daddy was scared of things. He carried a gun. Daddy couldn't protect me . . . but I don't think it matters anymore.

(*Lights from above go out fast, then come up one by one.*) Did you see that? . . . You can count the stars. . . .

Excerpt from *Tumor*

SHEILA CALLAGHAN

SARAH, late 20s, is two months pregnant.

SARAH: Walking around the women's department in Macy's. There are children everywhere, crawling like arachnids, they have more legs than I thought children were supposed to have but I guess you start to notice these things when you've been hijacked. Looking over their sweaty heads for something simple and angora I recall when angora was simple, when the angora gaze was not flecked with knots of unfiltered mess who run for no reason and stick to everything and wail like original sin multiplied by twelve.

I keep my eyes a safe distance above the swarming ick and spot a garment worthy of my once-upon self. I move towards it as smooth as a rollerball pen. Soon I am close enough to attract its static cling. My hand, electric, rises to the rising sweater arm, also electric, and in our dual reaching pose we are an Italian Renaissance masterpiece. But as my fingers splay for the grasp I feel an icy sludge make its way down my left leg.

I hear this: "It's not my fault, the bottom fell out!" And then a small person is galloping away from me towards a larger person. I look. My entire calf from knee to ankle is covered in a seeping red liquid. Pooling into the side of my sneaker is roughly eight ounces of bright red smashed ice. And lying next to my foot is a Slurpie cup with its bottom in shreds.

That night I dream of buckets and buckets of blood gushing from between my legs.

One Wasp

ELENA CARRILLO

EVA *is a woman, 25–45, in a freshly cleared-out space with only a can of bug repellent, a flashlight, a tall kitchen trash can, and an unopened can of sardines. She takes a deep breath to compose herself before she speaks.*

EVA: A wasp got into the house somehow. I just finished cleaning, throwing stuff out. It wasn't a yellow jacket. It was one of those big black ones . . . buzzing loudly against the glass, making the pane resonate. I should have left it alone, but I was afraid of being stung. The buzzing was absolutely maddening. I didn't think. I just picked up the still-rolled newspaper, and thwacked the wasp right against the glass. I guess I was expecting it to smush up. I was surprised—even annoyed—when it didn't. It fell onto the sofa beneath the window and buzzed in circles furiously, wildly stinging the cushion and the empty air. And it wouldn't die. Its hard insect armor and the softness of the couch cushion meant that every blow I dealt just pissed the thing off even more. I hit it harder and harder . . . will you *just* die? Will you *please* just die? (*Pause*) One of its little back legs broke off. Its wings were all crumpled. Finally it grew still.

It's still alive. God. I thought I killed it, but it's still alive and now lost somewhere in the trash can where I tossed it, newspaper and all. I can't very well dump out the trash looking for it. (*She shakes the bag in the can a little and listens as the wasp vibrates against the plastic. She looks frantic, then sprays into the can with the mosquito repellent, which only makes the wasp angry. The buzzing grows louder, more painful.*) Die, die, you miserable thing! Die! (*Beat*) I'm not angry with the wasp for living. I'm angry for the absence of him. This would have been his job—to handle whatever creepy-crawly was trapped and dying in our trash can. Our trash can. (*She suddenly throws the aerosol into the trash can, looks satisfied.*)

Anything you don't want can be discarded.

(*Beat*)

Truth is, our marriage was a freak accident. There were signs, but we ignored them. You're supposed to have doubts, right? If you don't have doubts, then something must be wrong. You must not be seeing things clearly. You're deluding yourself. (*She picks up the can of sardines.*) There were the sardines. Sardines. Who the hell eats sardines? It's a canned meat, first of all, which should tell you right away that it's bound to be disgusting. Like that canned ham that makes those sticky-kissy noises as it schlooops out onto the plate. It's like dog food, okay? And all right, I eat tuna, yes, it's true. But tuna is the end result of a lot of processing and when it gets to you, it just looks like a bunch of meat—you can't tell where the head and tail once were. Tuna also smells infinitely less fishy.

(*She studies the can, finally concedes.*) Okay, so it was a petty gripe, but stinking up the house with sardine plates and sardine cans was only part of it. . . . See, he would come home, drunk—which is fine; I never had a problem with him going out once in a while and having a good time. He liked to go out and play pool. He and his buddies would lay bets on every play of the game. Stupid bets. He'll make the shot, he won't make the shot, if he makes the shot, you have to tell the male waiter that you think he has a nice ass—that sort of thing, you know? And there was plenty of drinking involved. Always tequila shooters and choice beers for the winners, watered tap specials for the losers. I never knew whether he was winning or losing, he got trashed pretty much the same. Then he'd come home, stagger into the kitchen, grind open a can of sardines and bring them to *bed*. To *bed*, okay? I mean, it was bad enough when he ate them with crackers and onions at the kitchen tables, but to *bed*? And there's me, roused out of my sweet slumber by an odor you can't *even* begin to imagine. I flip on the light, and there he is! He's sitting up in bed—fully dressed because he's too smashed to get his shoes off—and he's eating sardines out of the can *with his fingers*!

I would lay there in the half-dark, listening to him slurp down the sardines, one after the next. Sluuurp, chew chew. Sluuuuurp, chew chew. Gulp. Ugh! My skin crawled. I clutched my laundry-fresh pillowcase under my nose. Smell the garden-fresh scent, I'd tell myself. Smell the clean freshness. But all I smelled was sardines. He'd pitch the can into the garbage can. Kerplunk, went the tinny emptiness. And then he'd snore. And I would lay there in the dark, trying to smell through all that stinky fishy smell while he snored 'til morning. Szzzzzzxxxxxxx. Szzzzxxxxxxxxxx. 'Til the alarm went off.

I could not believe he was gone. For a long time. Went 'round and 'round in my head in perfect denial. Then the bed grew cold and the dishes went unwashed and the newspaper . . . the newspaper went unread. So I used it to kill a wasp. (*She looks in the trash can sadly.*)

It's dead now. I haven't heard from it, so I think it's safe to say I killed it. (*Beat*) I killed it. It's just one measly wasp. But that's a hard thing to say. (*She takes up the sardine can and almost starts to speak, then changes her mind. She moves to throw the can away. She finds that she can't. She is very emotional as she grinds the can.*) The real denial was not seeing . . . all the time we'd been married . . . had been a fugue of some sort. Not mine or his, just a shared hysteria. And it only *seemed* to have been suddenly all gone in an instant when actually it had been fading out for years. (*She finally gets the can open. She takes a deep inhale. She reels back from the smell. She laughs and goes to throw the can of sardines in the trash, still finds it difficult, pulls the key off, tosses the can, and looks at the key, resigned.*)

I won't miss the sardines.

(*She ties the plastic bag at the top and then breathes deep, enjoying the fresh emptiness of the space. She pockets the tin key, smiling sadly.*)

But I will miss the snoring.

Pizza Apostrophe

KATHERINE CATMULL

A woman alone on stage, perhaps sprawled disconsolately on some furniture. Silence. She looks at her watch.

O pizza guy. I am starving. (*Pause. A new posture.*) Jesus CHRIST. (*Pause. Posture of despair.*) O pizza guy. I am so hungry. (*Pause*) I am so lonely. (*Pause*) Pizza guy. My heart is a hole, a whole circle, extra large with extra cheese, my cheesy dripping heart. Come see me. Bring your hot savory crust, bring your scarlet spicy sauce, bring a 32-oz. Coke with that.

O pizza guy hear the empty echo in my heartless stomach, in my stomachless heart, you could sing opera in there, you could fit a symphony in there. Let my echoing emptiness be a symphony to you.

O pizza guy don't make me talk, talking's bad luck for me, I'll get the order wrong. No, Christ I did not want anchovies with that! Oh how could you not tell from the ache in my voice that I wanted extra cheese! Know, just know, my deepest wants, the blackest richest saltiest olives, the woodsiest mushrooms, the crispiest little bits of pepperoni.

O but pizza guy, please want to hear my voice, though I might not speak. Cherish my whispered indecision, thick crust, no, thin crust, no: thick! No skimping with the foundation of our pizza, make it dense and solid. Then make another one you spin in the air and catch on your hand and look to see if it made me smile.

O pizza guy don't just bring a little, bring a lot, bring armloads of boxes, bring stacks of steaming savory pies of every kind; have more in the car. Never run out. Bring me obscure pizzas, exotic pizzas, with your best meats and rarest vegetables. Bring pizzas from Bali, topped with gaudy red flowers—bring

Tibetan pizzas, with yak butter for cheese, pizzas that melt away when the summer comes. O bring a pizza heaped with candied apple, quince, and plum, and gourd, with jellies smoother than the creamy curd, and lucent syrups, tinct with cinnamon. (*Pause*) Man that does sound good.

Bring me your own favorite pizza. Surprise me. (*Silence*)

O pizza guy, bring your own sweet whole self, and I won't need any dessert. (*Silence*)

I haven't actually ordered a pizza. (*Pause*) I think he's coming anyway. (*Pause*)

Recently my own choices haven't worked out so well. I thought maybe I would let someone else decide this time. I thought maybe the universe.

So I didn't call.

But I think he'll come.

O pizza guy come when I need you, not when I call. Be the universe knowing what I need right now, right now. Let Dear Abby be wrong when she says neediness is unattractive, because I am a fountain of neediness tonight, a geyser of need surrounded by giant spotlights: there! Neediness! Look! Ahhhhhhhhh! Ohhhhhh. Let my need be a siren instead. Not the policeman kind, the Odysseus kind, the kind on the rock with a song. Let my hunger be curvy, be sexy, with long hair, with a pearl bra and a scaly tail, singing to you, my needing song. How irresistible my hunger could be to a man with a car full of pizza and nowhere to go but here, here, here. My hunger will fit your pizza like another skin, we'll make a new creature: my belly with your pizza inside it.

O pizza guy don't hate my hunger! Don't be repulsed by my empty becrumbed and mustard-smeared refrigerator! I meant to go the store this week, I did! Only something came up, a call a question a job, something. The traffic was awful. I'm a terrible cook! Come to me smiling with your armfuls of boxes and whisper in my ear "we will never run out." Have parmesan tucked in your shirt pocket to make me smile. Don't forget to kiss me.

Pizza guy, make our pizza as carefully as a monk makes a sand mandala. Every sprinkle of cheese, every red pepper flake, all of it charged with intention and light!

Although.

I guess this means opening the door.

I guess I wasn't thinking that . . . I mean I wish you and the pizza would just . . . join me here. Do I definitely have to open the door? Couldn't you . . .(*Looks around the room.*) . . . no.

It's just, when you open the door, there's the wind and cold and . . . nature, and—

See actually I don't like the doorway. To be perfectly frank. I don't like thresholds, I don't like liminality, I don't like edges. I say I like the edge—man—but I don't. I want to be either Here or There. I don't want to be caught in between. I want what's coming to GET HERE, good or bad; I want what's come to never go away. I want to Be There Then. Or, you know: there. But not teetering on the precipice of this eternal now now now.

Do you know what the Tao is? A doorway! A gate! A gate you're eternally passing through, an endless threshold—the Infinite Teeter! A doorway you stand in forever, awaiting some cosmic pizza! Those Taoists are fucking nuts!

But I guess that's what it means, if you come. I'd have to stand in the doorway. I mean: there's no way around it.

That's where the pizza is.

Hmmm.

Naked in the doorway.

Well: effectively I would be.

Well I might as well be.

Well I would feel that way!

Oh hell. Because through that doorway you'll come and through that doorway you'll GO and in that doorway I will stand forever as everything rushes through and around and past me. One hungry Taoist!

And what if, what if you FLING the pizza at me angrily!

What if you don't take a check!

And what if, what if the pizzas cost too much, all the money I have, nothing left for me!

What if you bring your horrible friends and have a stupid giant pizza and beer bust right here in my living room and I can't go to sleep for days and you never leave and I have to move out and find a new house only I can't afford it the way prices have gone up around here and everything is ruined and I end up in some wretched little smelly room without even a CAT just lying on my bed too depressed to move let alone order pizza, until I wither away.

What if I'm scared.

Don't come, don't come! Pizza guy don't come! I am out of cash anyway, I am too fat to eat. My skin is breaking out. You will have bad breath. You will bring the wrong order, it will have Canadian bacon, I hate Canadian bacon, please don't come! Drive past the house, I will turn out the lights, I will hide in a closet. I would really rather have toast!

Skip it! God! Cancel the order! Oh doorbell don't ring, don't ring, don't ring. I don't know how much to tip! Just, just leave me here alone with my toast. (*Brief pause. Doorbell. More urgent, double doorbell. A very slow complicated smile dawns, from small to quite big.*)

The Risen Chris

VICKI CAROLINE CHEATWOOD

CHRIS, renegade trophy wife, has been tossed out of a bar for fighting. She's talking to Nero, the bouncer.

CHRIS: Dick's got this hang-up about his toenails. Toenails must be perfectly smooth, and shiny, at all times. He can't wear closed-toed shoes because he says his toenails can't breathe. This isn't something he popped on me after we got married, okay? I *knew*. He wore sandals with his tuxedo. Our wedding pictures have little glare spots on them. . . . He turned 64 this year. Every normal man his age is out screwing younger women. Things are really starting to slip, you know, physically too, and he doesn't know how to communicate, so every word that comes out of his mouth is toxic. Little toads. Little toads. You know that fairy-tale? When the good girl speaks, jewels fall out of her mouth, and when the bad girl speaks, little toads and snakes come out. Fourteen years of toads. (*Beat*) He'd been yelling at me for *two hours*. We'd gone to a party, and no one had talked to him, and it was my fault because . . . He's yelling at me, circling. I'm sitting in the chair, listening hard, trying to find something to grab on to, but he's belligerent. Raging. His face goes to purplish-black, and when he can't think of anything to say, he lunges and screams in my face. I'm thinking, "This is the day. This is the day I leave here in a bodybag." I'm already gone. I'm *ready* to go. There was pink foam coming out of his mouth, and I looked down at my suit and it was peppered with blood. He had screamed at me for so long that a blood vessel burst in his throat. There was blood, and foamy pink spit all over both of us. On my hands, my face. His blood . . . I went nuts. Years of being afraid, and *I* nearly kill *him*. The best fucking day of my life. (*Small laugh/gasp*) I scalped him. Cut out a notch of his scalp, round as an orange, from top of his forehead back beyond the hairline. Every single plug he had put in—I took 'em out. . . . I should have gone for toenails.

Excerpt from *Love Song for the Woman Whose Child Shot My Son*

PAULA CIZMAR

DEEANNE, a young woman whose ten-year-old son has been shot and killed by another ten-year-old, follows the mother of the shooter to work and fantasizes about getting to know her.

DEEANNE: Here's something. I got taken to a concert once. Some guy. I don't remember his name. It was classical music. People in suits. I guess he was trying to impress me or something. Very high falutin. I don't know Beethoven from . . . from—Well, look, I don't know nothing about none of it, so he didn't need to bother. We coulda gone for a coupla Coors or a movie and I still woulda put out. Not like I'm picky. Three dates a year—you know—Well. Whatever. Turns out he won the tickets anyway. Some call-in thing. Some radio station. He answered a question: What hit-TV-show family could claim perky petite Florence Henderson as Mom? That was the exact question. He kept telling me. That much I remember. Guess it was his favorite show. Watched a lotta late night cable. Meanwhile, he tells me later he thought the prize was gonna be tickets to *Phantom of the Opera* or something like that. But no, it was this thing. Classical.

So anyway, he takes me to the concert and he looks good. Wore a jacket. Maybe a tie. I don't remember. So I sat there. I was trying to appreciate it. I was trying to, uh—. Look, I woulda been happy with something I could hum along to, ya know? So at the intermission thing, I see this woman. Sitting next to a guy in a wheelchair. He's not that old. Neither is she.

But he can't move—that's pretty clear. She's sipping a coffee, sitting on a bench close to him. And all of a sudden she leans over, reaches out her hand, just real gentle, and wipes the drool from his lips. No need to mince words. It was fucking drool. And she wipes it away. No big deal, no comment, no calling attention to it. Just a gentle stroke of her hand. And I think—that's something only a woman would do. Ya know? And then I think, Why? 'Cause a woman's a sucker? 'Cause a woman's a loser? 'Cause a woman's so desperate to have a guy she'll wipe drool. Or. Maybe. 'Cause a woman isn't going to leave, just 'cause someone's legs give out, a woman isn't going to leave at the first sign of trouble? I don't know. Maybe it's 'cause a woman knows the hell involved when you decide to really love.

That's all I got from that concert. Don't remember the guy. Don't even remember what the guy looked like. The music? Forget it. I just remember that woman and the tissue full of drool.

Daddy's Girl

VERONIQUE DE TURENNE

ANGELIQUE, an actress in her 30s, goes on a blind date.

ANGELIQUE: Shit, I'm late? I'm so sorry I'm late but my father died last week and my stepmother—that bitch—mailed him to me. The mailman comes walking up the driveway and has me sign for this package wrapped in duct tape. Careful, it's heavy, he says. My dad hasn't ever been to the house and now here he is, in this ratty little cardboard box. Jesus fucking Christ.

Put it in a good place, my brother said. What the hell does that mean? Do I put it on the desk my father gave me when he moved back to Paris? I can remember him signing my report cards at that desk in the house in Hollywood. Or how about the filing cabinet that still has the I'm-sorry-you're-sick-I-love-you letter I wrote in an Oprah moment? My friend Paula keeps her mother on a TV tray in the living room next to the VCR. I'm still not sure if that's supposed to be funny. But it turned out I couldn't bring the box into the house at all, so I left it on the porch overnight.

My brother and sister had a fight with Dad before he left and they're still mad at him. But I miss him. I want to talk about how tall he was, and how elegant. He could make jeans and a T-shirt look like a tux. I want to hear about how everyone on the set always wound up hanging out in his production office, drinking beer and telling dirty jokes, and how he sounded just like Jacques Cousteau but with a better vocabulary. Once, when this asshole director dropped him off at the house after a meeting Dad said, "I'd invite you in but I'm afraid you'd accept." But you know who's the only person who wants to talk about that stuff? The bitch. My stepmother. How is that fair?

This morning was the memorial service. My brother decided to go to a retreat on the Russian River because he needs to get in touch with his anger. I think all vegans are a little bit angry. I mean, all that tofu. My sister canceled because her miniature horse has projectile diarrhea. Don't ask. So I decorated my kayak with French lavender from the garden and paddled out, way far out to where you can't hear any sounds from the shore and I emptied the box with Dad in it into the Pacific Ocean. God. The ashes hissed as they went into the water, and then they drifted in the current and turned the water this amazing shade of blue. I just sat there and let it surround me. Then it was gone and I paddled back and that was that.

So, tell me about your family.

Years Ago

LISA DILLMAN

A woman, in her mid-60s, wears a ratty old robe and looks as if she hasn't slept well for some time. Silence for a moment.

A house. White—no! Graying white. With a graying green roof. My house once. A man. Prominent chin. A nose—hmm . . . how would one describe that nose? A nose . . . many times broken. Underbite. An underbite leaves the impression that the person is constantly smiling. But this man. Didn't smile often. He always had a reason. He didn't smile when I tried to make him smile. He only smiled—if there was a reason. But . . . what was I saying? A house. White. *No.* Not white. I always want things to be white. But the house. The house was graying white. In the kitchen . . . a big table . . . my mother's. She gave it to me. When I got married. She's not dead. She lives far away. In the Midwest. Where the sky is mostly gray. Whatever happened to my mother's big table? (*Beat*) Near the table, a counter. Littered with food and toys and a roach motel. On the floor at the end of the counter, four six-packs of Pepsi. Empty. Just sitting there. The man. The man drinks Pepsi in place of wine. He did. In those days. Pepsi. His sweet, syrupy vice. I remember . . . once I told a neighbor woman that at least he wasn't a drinker. Amidst the storm of my complaint against him I tossed in that tiny lifeboat. I thought of him and his six-a-day of Pepsi, and I said flat out at least he isn't a drinker. I felt just as if I were telling a lie, but of course she assumed I meant liquor. Pepsi. Lots of things were important, but I didn't know. (*Beat*) That woman—the neighbor lady—we used to spend Thursday evenings together. Drinking. All kinds of strange and wonderful mixtures. Kahlua and cream. Amaretto and orange juice. Old Bushmills with a beer back. I told her lots of stories on those

Thursday nights. Sometimes I told her the truth but that was rare and I had to be pretty tight. I told her I'd been an actress. That the man hit me when the kids made too much noise. That he hung my cat, Chiggers, from the shower rack just to watch it kick. She—poor woman—wanted to get the police after him. I always stopped her from doing anything. Because he really was a . . . a good man. And because I was lying. I never had a cat. (*Beat*) I think it was my idea to have separate bedrooms. . . . Yes, I'm sure it was. *First*, it was my idea. Then he seemed to like it. That made me mad—I said I wanted a divorce. He said he wanted a separation. Then we separated. Then he wanted a divorce. He told me while I was visiting him one weekend. I was visiting . . . to tell him I'd come back. If he wanted. I . . . because I missed him, our life. Our . . . marriage. I didn't want anyone else. And he had the boy. Our son. I had the two girls . . . oh. . . . (*Beat*) He'd met someone. I had too. But I didn't care. I wanted to be back. I wanted to be back in the white house—the *graying* white house! God damn it. He told me I was smarter than he was. Deserved better. Needed a career. Needed to *succeed* at something—anything—my *music* even. He was so . . . kind. Hugging me. We made love that night—like we had just met—just fallen in love—and I thought: There! That's how it's supposed to be and we're both so smart and so young and so good-looking and there's every reason why. . . . In the graying white house that night I woke up, reached for him. To tell him. I wanted to stay married, that of course it was the only thing that mattered. . . . But in the thin gray dawn, the man . . . the man had left our bed. He had slipped down the hall to the other bedroom. What had once been *my* bedroom. And when I tiptoed to the doorway, I heard his breathing. Deep. Relaxed. Divorced. Yes. A . . . graying white house . . . with a graying green roof. My house. Once.

The Cassandra Complex

LINDA EISENSTEIN

CASSANDRA *is a woman old enough to know better. Her demeanor is somewhere between a rat-a-tat standup comic and an intense performance artist. She wears a mix of ancient Greek and contemporary dress—a laurel wreath and a toga, say, over tight jeans with bright red high-top sneakers.*

CASSANDRA: I have totally given up talking to men. Totally. I mean, men never listen. At least they never listen to me. They haven't believed one of my prophecies in the last, say, thirty-two hundred years. Not that I have anything new to say to them anyway. I've said it all before. Everything starts to sound like the worst recycled crap. I mean, I used to shout at Agamemnon until I was hoarse, it never did either of us a damn bit of good. It's just, I thought this reincarnation would be better. There were so many promising signs. First the sixties, then another wave of feminism, then the New Age, and finally: the Information Age.

So I told myself: listen, Cassandra. This time, be smart. Forget oracles for the ruling class. So what if the Big Guys won't listen to you? Times have changed. Go right to the viewing audience. Direct marketing. Infomercials. Cable TV. Nowadays a woman doesn't have to be pleasant or accommodating to be successful at this game. Hell, look at Susan Powter. Write yourself a self-help book and promote the bejesus out of it. So I did. And here it is, my masterpiece: Forget Electra, Cinderella, Sleeping Beauty, Wendy. This syndrome is old as the hills of Troy, and worse for you, too. I've suffered from it for several unspeakable millennia, and so have you, ladies. Suffered from: (*Holding up a book*) "The Cassandra Complex."

The Cassandra Complex. Never heard of it? But you KNOW this baby, you know it to the bone. This is the one where you tell it like it is and they ignore you because you're a woman, and then when it comes true they either a) don't remember you predicted it or b) blame you for it like you made it happen or c) call you a witch and kick your ass. Yeah. The Cassandra Complex. The most dangerous disease in the world. So I've been doing the TV talk show circuit. And even with this book, this fabulous useful book full of prophecies—I mean, come on! You gotta love the damn thing, how could you not? Oracles older than Nostradamus, secrets channeled straight from the mouth of the Godhead, nothing but 3000 years of a woman's stone-ass truth—there's still this big problem.

They get me on the show. Schmeer on the makeup. Clip on the microphone. Zoom in the camera. The host comes out: (*A glowing insincerity, as a talk-show hostess*) "And now, a special treat. You've read her book. And you didn't like it. Well, here she is, direct from the smoldering ruins of that once-great city of Troy: let's give a big L.A. welcome to the prophetess Cassandra, the woman nobody likes to hear."

Oh, shit, oh boy, they all think, here it comes, here it comes, the rant, that horrible rant, and they can feel the engine rev as I start to speak, hear Apollo's gift descending upon us all, and I begin to prophesy, and adders and fiery letters and burning truth come pouring out of me, pouring out in a hot golden gush, like molten lava, like napalm visions from the heart of Kali-Ma—and—

No one hears it. No one hears a single word. They think they're going to hear it, and a switch clicks in their head, that self-protecting switch—and they shunt it away. I've just done a performance that nobody heard. Oh, they think they heard me. In their minds they substitute a facsimile speech, one they've heard before, turn it on automatic, and go out to lunch. La la la, rant away, babe, I'm thinking about my laundry now.

Why does it happen, this joke of Apollo, this so-called gift of mine that only seems to plug up people's ears? I've tried and tried to figure it out. What makes them not hear me? I used to think it was fear or ignorance or bigotry. Then I thought it was hatred, sheer hatred of women. But after three thousand years? I just don't know. My latest theory is that maybe it's the pitch of my voice, that whine of the supercharged motor that makes it a rant and not even the words. Is it the frequency itself that makes them turn that little switch? It can't be the content—God knows they never get far enough into it to actually HEAR the freaking content.

And for all those people who've been saying I'm a "man-basher," a man-hater? Man-hater! Now there's a joke! Over all those centuries? I loved men. My unforgivable sin, the sin that really made Apollo curse me? It was trying to help him too much. Whenever I loved a man, really cared about him and his ideals and his little projects, you couldn't keep me quiet. I couldn't keep my mouth shut. I'd be buzzing around, full of energy, always giving advice, perfectly willing to be the helpmate, perfectly willing to be the power behind the throne, never even looking for face time. Well, okay, but I only led the army that one time, one time!—during my Joan years. And did the little weasel appreciate it? Hah! Just one more life up in smoke.

So I'm changing my ways. I'm gonna keep my mouth shut, stay out of trouble. And you women out there? I hate to say this, but maybe you should too. Mark my words. Guys really get a hard-on for I-told-you-so dames. You gotta pretend you didn't see it coming, like it was an accident they got fired, or demoted, or usurped, when as far as you could see the handwriting was blazing away on the wall. It's not safe when you can read the messages that clear.

You know, if men would actually listen when some Cassandra speaks, they'd gain so much, so much more than they'd lose, but for so many guys, it's just not in their constitution. You tell the truth, read the runes, see the future barreling toward 'em right there in the tea leaves, but if you say anything, they kill the messenger for sure. Don't expect any gratitude—it's not gonna come. You want recognition for good works? Put a copper in the Salvation Army kettle but don't try to save a man from his fate.

Hell, maybe it's not even their fault—that they don't know how to sail without armor and spikes on their shoes and plugs in their ears. That's the world they live in. That hateful, armored, nothing-but-enemies-and-loud-noises world. And that world, dear friends, is the world I refuse to speak to any more.

(*She begins to exit, then turns around in frustration.*) And the thing that kills me is . . . I know the secret. The one that could save us all. I mean, I'm a goddamn oracle, okay? Ya know, mouthpiece of the deity? Infallible? Ask me anything! It's in here. It's the truth, goddamn it! Why doesn't anybody believe me? (*Throughout the following, the sound of her voice fades, then abruptly cuts out—as though someone has pressed a "mute" button.*) You people, you NEVER change, you never listen, and you could all be saved, why the hell don't you ever believe a thing I say. . . .Why can't you hear me? (*Cassandra continues moving her lips and waving her arms excitedly, as the lights fade.*)

Hay

CYNTHIA FRANKS

GIDA, 40s–50s, walks out of an old falling down farmhouse. She carries a suitcase and a handful of yellow straw. She speaks to the audience.

GIDA: Hay is an emotional crop. Wheat, soy, you put them in the ground when you should and barring a weather catastrophe, you harvest them in the fall when it's time. But hay—hay's a crop fraught with emotion. Each decision is life or death. Your people ever put in hay?

Life or death. When to plant? When to cut? The hay wagons, the bailer, how many people you need to bring it in. . . . The weather—always matching wits with the weather. Weather usually wins. Cutting's what puts most people over the edge. You ever cut hay? So many, many things can go wrong. We don't do hay anymore. Not since Mother passed. Each decision could mean no crop at all, your livestock starves or freezes. Life or death. If you cut on the wrong day and it doesn't dry right, you could burn your barn down.

You don't think it can happen? I'm here to tell you it can. Seen it. You bet your sweet pututti, from hay. Like compost. It gets hot in the middle. Ferments. It gets hot from the breaking down. The stuff on the outside of the bail is dry—Poof! No barn. That's why you don't keep your stock and your hay in the same place. And if it rains after you cut, forget it. All gone. That's why you cut half and half. You at least end up with half a crop. Half's better than nothing. You know the guy from the humane society thought this was hay? Can you believe it? How can someone who doesn't know the difference between hay and straw be caring for my babies? They just come in here and took 'em. Can't tell hay from straw.

Yeah, hay is an emotional crop. If you cut at the right time, mid July give or take, it's the hottest four days of the year. You're out there working in a flannel shirt and your heaviest jeans. Hay'll rip your skin to shreds. Feel that. Imagine that on the tender part of your arm? Everyone's hot. Everyone's irritable. Something breaks down and everyone's got an opinion how to fix it. And everyone's positive they're right.

My mother—there was a woman who knew hay. You know there's not a man on this planet knows how a knotter works. The thing that ties the hay bales. They think they know, but they don't. The knotter and bail twine were invented by Balen Cordage Company. That's why they're called hay bales. That's what Ma told me. Don't know if it's true. Don't care. I like to think it's true. The knotter's a complicated mechanism. A complete mystery, like the weather. My mother could fix 'em. She had the gift; and about the weather too. People were always coming over here to get her to fix their knotters. Ask anyone around here, they'll tell you. Vivian Thornton knew her knotters. Well, any of us oldies, not these cry-baby farmer wannabes, "I want city water, I want piped gas, horses smell funny." Really burns my butt!

Next thing we'll have sidewalks. Over my dead body will they put a sidewalk in front of my house. Stay in a place long enough and the city will move to you. That's why they come and took my babies: my horses, my lambs, my little dogs. These city people moving in. People around here know there's nothing wrong with the way I keep my babies. Kennel license. My mother didn't need a kennel license. More then five dogs and it's the law. "You don't have a proper facility. You can't keep them."

What's wrong with my house? What's wrong with my barn? So it leans. It's leaned like that for fifty years. They're little dogs. And people who think hay is straw are caring for them. Terriers, smart as a whip. Hard to train. Then there's my Seldon. My horse. I was a young girl when Seldon came into my life. They said he'd never live. I knew. Hay was good that year. Got the whole crop in—dry, fresh, young. He was getting thin. 'Cause he's dying. Not 'cause I didn't care for him. It's his time. A horse lives on a place almost forty years, he should be allowed to die there. Well . . . guess it's time to go. (*Picks up suitcase.*) Hay . . . is an emotional crop . . .

An American Lamp

MELISSA GAWLOWSKI

*A woman is in the studio audience of a televised infomercial; the
host has approached her for a testimonial about the product.*

Now, I just wanted to say that this lamp has done wonders for
my home. See, I used to have this unofficial competition going
with my neighbor, Francine, where we were always trying to see
who could own the most items in memory of the late Princess
Diana, God rest her soul. Now, I had the plates, the dolls, coins,
salt and pepper shakers—you name it, I had it. Except for that
hubcap that Francine came up with, probably out of some junk
yard, but she claimed was from *the* car. From the accident. I'll
tell you right here, though, that it was clearly a fake—*that's right,
I said it, Francine*! But anyway, everything changed when 9/11
hit, y'know? I had a real realization about it then, that sorta
"What am I doing," y'know? Now, I loved Lady Di, and I still
do, but what good did it do to buy items to commemorate her
tragic demise? That's no way to live your life. So I threw all
those Diana goods away, that's right, and I started spending my
money in a more practical way—buying things to remember
September 11th instead. Everyone says I have the most patriotic
home in the neighborhood, and I'm not ashamed to say that
boy, is Francine burning mad that she didn't think of it first. So,
yes, mister, I love my lamp, and I say to you, God Bless America!

A Day in the Death of Sheldon Wasserman

LAURIE GRAFF

A courtroom. An actress has been subpoenaed for jury duty. She appeals to the judge.

ACTRESS: I'm sorry, Your Honor, but I don't feel I can serve on this jury. I just can't be responsible for this. I am a very sensitive person. I'd be up nights wondering whether or not I did the right thing. Who am I to decide the fate of Sheldon Wasserman? And what kind of name is that for a murderer? Bugs, Kapo, Cheeks . . . That's a murderer. Sheldon? "Sheldon, if I told you once I told you a thousand times—No Murder!" I'm sorry, your Honor . . . See, the defense attorney said Sheldon did not murder his wife Carol of forty years in their Upper East Side apartment in the middle of the night. He just killed her. Excuse me, but I'm supposed to lose money and miss work so I can differentiate between murder and killing. And if he's not found guilty of murder in the second degree, beyond a reasonable doubt, Shelly could actually be free to go home, have a cup of tea, and call it a day. A bad day, but still . . . Temporary insanity? Let me ask you—how many hours does temporary insanity last? Does it last, say . . . long enough to bludgeon the skull of your wife with a golf club, stab her eight times, get her into a wardrobe box and put her out with the garbage? Wouldn't you think that somewhere between the second stab and ringing for the elevator some sanity had to snap back? Something had to be cooking to get her past the doorman and onto York Avenue. Something must have clicked with the decision to drive to New Jersey and bury her in the building behind work. There has to be some level of sanity just to get across the George Washington Bridge. The only

45

moment where sanity was suspended was in his decision to use the putter. And what was Shel thinking during the car ride— "Gee, Carol, I never really liked your pot roast"? Forty years ago Carol came home from a date, called up a girlfriend and said, "I met him. He's a dream. His name is Sheldon. This is IT!" What went wrong? Maybe Carol was a castrating bitch who had poor Sheldon by the balls. Maybe she was a rich adulteress who drove him to Prozac and booze and murder—I mean killing. What happens to people? When is it safe? When can you really know? After forty years you'd think Sheldon and Carol knew. You see, Your Honor, for a hopeful, romantic, single girl who already has problems seeing a man up for murder who looks like her Uncle Moe, and reminds her of someone who sits in the back row of the temple, this is a tough pill to swallow. Perhaps it's all pre-destined, maybe you just have to get lucky. I don't know. I don't have the answers, so please, Your Honor, do us all a favor and don't pick me for this jury.

My Mother

ELLEN HAGAN

A young girl talking with her mother about sex for the first time.

My mother and I spent the night talking about sex. It's funny to
me, how in a conversation over baked potato soup, hot rolls
with skinny packets of butter, iceberg lettuce salad with day-old
croutons and honey mustard dressing, chicken fingers and barbecue sauce at a Bob Evans in Clarksburg, West Virginia, my
mother and I suddenly feel the need to discuss sex and orgasm
and she knows and I know, and it's about as uncomfortable as I
think I will ever get. My mother and I, sharing sweet tea and
oral sex! Ha! Who the fuck knew, huh?

And get this, my mother says, out loud in the motherfuck-
ing Bob Evans, "I don't mean to brag, but in 53 years, I have
never once had sex without an orgasm, and I am telling you
right now Addie, that I don't intend to." Bam, just the fuck like
that! I nearly wet my pants and snorted up barbecue through
my nose. And she is my mother! And all of a fucking sudden,
over goddam biscuits and gravy and pork roll and ham hock and
every other redneck delicacy this side of the Appalachians. She
is woman. She is sexual. She has a vagina and she has been using
it. She has sex and she is my mother. Sick, is what I think and
then at the same time, I don't know what to think. She tells me
I should not be sleeping with who I am sleeping with. I think I
agree with her, but goddamn, how do you think it is that I am
supposed to stop all of this, huh? I gotta get outta this thing that
I am up to my neck into.

A woman is not a receptacle. My mother said that tonight.
She said a woman is not a safety deposit box, not a safe you keep
shit in. She is not a grocery cart. When you put the key back in,
a quarter doesn't pop out. My mother became a fleshy woman

47

tonight, and I knew and the waitress knew, and the man who was sitting next to my mother, who we said was getting a real earful, knew. Hallelujah! I think.

Excerpt from *Marathon Dancing*

LAURA HARRINGTON

JULIET is 16, the youngest contestant in the dance marathon. She is a circus performer, a high wire walker. She comes from a famous family of high wire walkers.

JULIET:
One time I was performing with my father.
Our signature show.
We're on a wire over an outdoor stadium in Oakland,
California.
Clear skies. Light wind. Not bad.

He stops in the middle and cooks an omelet over this little
coal stove he's been carrying on one shoulder.
I have to eat it, of course.
That's part of the act.
It's never cooked enough.
I can't eat eggs anymore.

I'm on a unicycle.
He passes me the skillet and a fork.
I take a bite. And he falls.
My mouth is full of runny eggs. And he falls.
Steps sideways like he's in his own kitchen.
There's no sideways on the wire.
There's the beginning and the end.
That's all.

Sideways. Like there's a nice worn linoleum floor under our feet.
Sideways. Like he's gonna get me a glass of milk to go with my eggs.

There was a second when he looked in my face.
He's stepped off the wire, his eyes are level with mine.
He's falling. And there's no surprise.
And then he's gone.
I can't even look down.
I can't look down or I'll follow him.
And the only thing I still know in that moment is that I don't want to fall.

I don't know how I got down.
I felt his hands helping me.
Impossible, my mind knows that.
But my body felt his hands.

Grace.
My father was full of grace.
Physically perfect.
Perfectly focused.
Think only of the wire and crossing to the end.
Think only of the wire . . .

Tigger

TIA DIONNE HODGE

In the year 1980, I was eight years old, and the world was full of third grades of blues and blondes. With smiling faces and white rolled down socks, Mrs. Hettinger's class would overflow with 8 A.M. morning glories as we'd find our seats within our flip-top desk world and head into another day of Math, Social Studies, and Science. And I was the only brown-brown among them. You know, the blue-blondes, sometimes green-browns, reds with freckles. . . . All ready for another chance to rectify themselves. I'd give them the chance to call me "Tia," without the other half: "She's the *Black* Girl," they'd say. Not Kara the smart one, Beth the short one, Sarah the pretty one, or even Scott—the goof—but "The Black Girl." I could have been Tia The Gymnast. I could do cartwheels that would stun Nadia Comaneci herself. I could have been Tia The Runner. I could outrun every last one of them. I could have been Tia The Artist, Tia The Singer, even Tia The Helper. I could out imagine, out sing and out help anyone . . . if they had asked. (*Beat*) But Holly still wouldn't let me Chinese jump rope with her at recess. You know: In, Out, Side-Side, On, In, Out. She'd make me stand alone. So, I got my own Chinese jump rope, stretched it between two chairs and practiced. (*Jumping*) In, Out, Side-Side, On, In, Out. In, Out, Side-Side, On, In, Out! Hey! In, Out, Side-Side, On, In, Out! Oh, I jumped and spun! Hopped and landed . . . On two feet, on one. I did highs and lows, skinnies and fatties, criss-crosses . . . Everything! Then one day, Holly's jump rope snapped. I saw them out of the corner of my eye as I did a high skinny. (*Jumping*) In, Out, Side-Side, On, In, Out. Some stood and said: "Well, Tia's looks fun . . . Maybe we should ask if we can play with her?" And that's when Holly said it. She said it cool, calm and to the point. "My Dad says I can't

51

play with Tiggers." (*Beat*) Now, they thought, pondered, and thought some more . . . and walked away from Holly and played with me that day. I became: Tia, The Chinese Jump Rope Queen! as we played, and Holly stood alone refusing my invitations. "My Dad says I can't play with Tiggers!" Didn't she know? I mean, couldn't she see? Even within our flip-top desk world of Math, Social Studies, and Science, didn't she see that Tiggers are wonderful things? They're bouncy, pouncy, founcy, flouncy, fun-fun-fun-fun-fun. The only other thing about Tiggers . . . is I'm the only one.

Ingerto (Plant Fusion)

QUIARA ALEGRIA HUDES

YUYITA PEREZ is elderly, with an astonishing hunch in her back. Born in Puerto Rico, she came to the United States in her 50s. Her accent is thick and luscious. She has just returned from the corner store and inspects the small avocado she purchased.

YUYITA: *Aguacates para hoy? Carajo, que sin verguenca!* That's the last time I'll buy anything from those people! They told me they had good *aguacate* and *mira!* This is as hard as my fake teeth. And it looks like an old man's wrinkled wee-wee. It's been over thirty years since I saw a wee-wee but I think it looked something like this. They should be ashamed to ask two dollars for this.

Ah ah ah. I want my vegetables to be big. In Puerto Rico I used to grow them myself. We called it *ingerto.* You mix two different plants together. You wedge one plant and tie it into place on another plant. I made an *aguacate* the size of a dog. Now that was an *aguacate.* People lined up to see that. One man drove all the way from the city and gave me twenty dollars for it. I made things you wouldn't believe. *Guayabas* that came out white and yellow. Garlic that smelled like a rose. That was an aphrodisiac. People begged me, "More garlic. More garlic." But you see? . . . Sometimes your special gifts cause you the biggest problems. My husband kept eating the garlic. He became very horny. One day I walked into the house and he was doing it with my cousin on the couch. I took off my *chancletas* and smacked his naked butt and hers too. Ay, I left some good bruises there. Sometimes your special gifts cause you the biggest problems.

53

Excerpt from *Take a Powder*

LINDSAY BRANDON HUNTER

It's a hideout, sometimes, no question. But when you really need a break from the world? The bathroom is always there. You can be in the middle of a wedding, you can be on the dance floor, in a museum, in a staff meeting, you can be in the middle of the best date movie of 1992, slightly touching Michael Bertoucci's left hand inside the popcorn bucket—and if you feel so uncomfortable that your blood becomes carbonated and your tongue expands so large it threatens to grow limbs and become its own mammal: you excuse yourself.

There are some situations in which it's not that easy. I avoid all of them. Horseback riding, mountain climbing, childbirth, suicide hotline operation, cardiac surgery, public performance, marathons, fire fighting, race car driving, most team sports. Being in the wilderness does pose difficulty. But ninety percent of the time, you can announce your sudden departure for the little girls' room at any moment, and even if it poses an inconvenience, no one is going to deny you. No one, no one except maybe the very most heartless, can fault you for going to the bathroom. They won't even ask you *why*. They don't want to hear it. And even if there are suspicions, no one is so petty as to outright impugn your motivation for visiting the toilet, for god's sake. Think what they like, in any given situation it's entirely possible that you might have to pee. You always have a get-out-of-life-free card, at least for ten minutes.

Mrs. Pugh

SANDRA HUNTER

MRS. PUGH is a cleaning lady with a working-class London accent. She is dressed in cleaning clothes, hat, glasses and sensible shoes. She is going to tell you How Things Are.

MRS. PUGH: On Monday mornings I clean Mr. Skipp's place. He's a young bloke, and I don't know what he does with hisself, but his hair's leaving him. It's everywhere—like great big drifts of snow across the Russian steppes—except it's black.

When I got there last week, I could see he'd been shedding again. I turned off the vacuum cleaner so's I could shout a bit better. "The hair," Mr. Skipp, "the hair—I can't be expected to spend my life following the follicles of your youth." 'Course he didn't hear, did he? He was in the front room yogering [yoga-ing]. He does that most mornings, lying there in the abalone position, being at one with his stocks and shares. I don't know why they do it, I really don't. If the good lord had meant us to yoger (*Beat*) he wouldn't of give us back problems, would he?

So he's yogering, while I'm grouting all this hair out from under the sink. His hair gets everywhere. I've found it stuck on the mirror, wound around his computer cables. He spends all day in front of that computer. I told him I said, "What you need is a real job." He said he likes working alone. I said, "No wonder you're so peculiar. You don't mix with no one, and you'll get worse, end up like that Nancy Perkins, completely potty." Now she stayed at home all her life. Her mum come home one afternoon and finds Nancy putting all her underwear in the blender. I said, "You being a researcher and all, you might want a little background information on people what never go out. Agromaniacs they're called." Nancy Perkins was one and look at her now. They can't take her out unless they put her on a leash.

Breaks your heart just to look at her, and imagine her old mum—what's it like for her? Ah, love her. Mr. Skipp says, "What I do requires a great deal of concentration." I said, "You ever been to Spain, Mr. Skipp? Three weeks of sand, sea, sun. (*Sings*) *Una paloma blanca*—I'm just a bird in the sky. A bit of a knees up—you know what a knees up is?" He don't look like his knees have been anywhere. Ah, love him.

So I'm cleaning the sink and I heard this moaning sound. First of all I thought he was singing his mantras, you know om—tiddly om pom or something. But then I heard him, "Mrs. Pugh—" I thought I better check up on him. He does pay me after all even if I do have to remind him. And there he is—well I say there he was because I knew it was him, but it didn't look like him. His bum was stuck up in the air and his face was all squashed up between his legs like he was giving birth to hisself. It give me a bit of a funny turn. He looked just like my dad did when he fell down the stairs. There was all this bump bump bump and this almighty crack and there he was base over apex, as you might say, stone dead.

So there's Mr. Skipp on the floor saying, all lah di dah, "Mrs. Pugh, I seem to have got myself into a bit of a pickle. Do you think you could give me a hand to get myself out of this?"

I been doing this job now for twenty-five years, and I've never been required to touch my employer except for one dirty old bugger, s'cuse my French, who tried to follow me into the bathroom while I was having a tinkle. He was foreign and they don't have the same bathroom habits like what we do. Still, you got to draw the line somewhere. I told him, I said, "We don't do that sort of thing in this country," but he kept coming at me. There's me with me unmentionables round me ankles. I stood up and give him a shove. He's a big fat bleeder, and he must of slipped or sunnink. He didn't half crack his head on the toilet. I don't like people touching me. He should've kept his hands to hisself. If he hadn't kept grabbing at me ankles, I wouldn't have kicked him so many times. I had me sensible shoes on, and I caught him a few good ones right under the chin. His head was smacking against the toilet. There was this crack and then sort of a wet mushy sound, like if you was to kick in a pineapple really hard. There was all this stuff coming out the back of his head. I kept aiming for the chin, you know, so's to keep me shoes clean. I find with appearances, it's the little things that count.

The police report said it was an accident. A bloke that size was courtin' disaster wearing silk slippers in the bathroom. I thought it was best they didn't know about me being in the bathroom at the time of the incident. You don't want that sort of thing getting back to the family. They sent the body back to his mum and dad in Turkey. I said if they wanted me to clean up that mess in the bathroom, they'd have to pay me extra on top of my normal wages.

Well, you got to look after yourself haven't you? Look at the rubbish I got to put up with here. Here I am with this 'uge apartment to clean, massive it is, enough rooms in there to put two or three of them big Indian families in. Anyway, there I am trying to do me cleaning and Mr. Skipp gets hisself all rubic-cubed. I said, "I got my hands all dirty trying to unclog the hair down your drain. You wait here while I finish up." I haven't had a raise in a year, so I left him to think about things for a bit.

He did remind me of me old dad, lying there. We was all there watching, except me mum—she was at the shops so she missed it. Sally, she's the youngest said, "Is he dead then?" Paul said, "I'm not touchin' 'im." Sally goes, "Why not—he touches you enough." I said, "That's enough of that." Being the eldest, I took charge. I sent them in the kitchen and told them to put the kettle on. I said I'd be along in a bit. I told him I said, "You lie there and think about things." I wouldn't have done nuffink but his chin was sticking out. I mean he was asking for it, begging for it. I used to wear sensible shoes in them days, too. They wasn't what you call fashionable, but they was useful in their way. Anyway, I didn't kick him much—just a few times—one for Paul, one for Sally, one for me old mum. He didn't say nothing, his head went all floppy. I went in the kitchen and made the tea. It was mum come back and started screaming. That's how we knew he was dead. Sad really.

Mr. Skipp's not bad to clean up after. At least he's not like that Mrs. Benito. Now she's a one for paying cash up front when she goes off to the Costa del Sol to work on her skin cancer, but I'm telling you, the woman's a nightmare. She says she's forty-three. I'm fifty-four. I know what forty-three-year-old women look like, and it's not her. Old Mrs. Benito always brings me a little something from the Costa del Sol. One year she brought me a bikini made of seashells. I thought it was one of them macrame things you hang from the ceiling. I told her, I said, "I can't go round with bits of string stuck up me bum at my time of life." She says, "You got to live a little." Ooh, sometimes I could hit her.

And talking about things getting stuck, I didn't forget about Mr. Skipp. After I did his kitchen, I come back and he managed to get hisself out of it without me having to touch him. He was all red and sweaty and he couldn't stand up for a while. I said, "What did you do that for?" He said, "It's meant to relax you." I didn't say a word. I did get my raise, though. Ah, love him.

Water Lilies

JULIE JENSEN

BELLA *is the unenthusiastic twin of a water ballet team member. She is talking to her sister, Betty, the other half of the team. They have just lost a competition—the Olympics.*

BELLA: This is the thing about water ballet. You repeat the same two minutes of your life over and over again, tens of thousands, if not millions, of times. And every time it is exactly the same, it looks the same, it is, for all intents and purposes, exactly the same, exactly the same! And then, preposterous as it may sound, someone else sits out there and judges it. This part was closer to the same, this thing was further from the same, and this is your grade for sameness. But even that is not the worst of it. The worst of it is the fact that this, this two minutes endlessly repeated, is the only thing that matters. The only thing about my life or my thoughts or any actions that matters. The only thing. Do you know what muscles in me are the most exhausted? Face. Face muscles. I have an exhausted face. From enjoying it so much.

Really, Betty, you're just afraid to hang up your nose plugs. You have serious doubts about whether you exist. If you're not doing a torpedo twirl and a military salute in some container of water, you may not be alive. What will become of you, I wonder, when repetition and grading are not a part of your day? Will you every morning make a thousand eggs and a thousand pieces of bacon? Trying to do each one just like the one before? Getting caught in endless strings of repetitions?

Well, not me. Not ever me. I want to go to the Goose Necks of the San Juan. Set up a little sun shade and live out my days as a desert animal with a view of the dry red earth. I will not swim again forever. I am going to save the desert tortoise. I'm going to collect cicada songs. I will live like a lizard on a red rock surrounded by juniper and sage. Me and all the dry creatures of the desert.

Angela

TANIA KATAN

*ANGELA, 30s, has been caught at the Laundromat sniffing a woman's
thong. She speaks to the thong owner.*

ANGELA: No, see I was doing you a favor, helping you out, lend-
ing a hand, extending a . . . look, some people, they like to
LOOK at the world, watch the world, sort of like a passive par-
ticipant, like, life is a Disney View Finder, just clicking their way
into prearranged scenery. A still-life situation. See, for these people, the thought of moving, of actually living the pictures, is just
too stifling to mentally sift through. There are others who prefer to listen, like you, for example, are listening to me right now.
Listeners are probably the most important people on the Senses
Train—they receive, process and then express themselves in a
calm, warm manner, like you . . . might do . . . tomorrow. There
are some other senses, but I can see how you might be interested
in getting to The Point so . . . I introduce my category, the
Olfactory folks. We want to taste the world through our noses,
nasal our way into your hearts, or your laundry, as the case may
be. We can't help it, it's not an action, action would imply
Thinking plus Movement. What I'm talking about is
Intoxication. Immersing plus Sinking or Diving plus Drowning.
As you can see, Intoxication lends itself naturally to many nau-
tical metaphors. Water and . . . something, seem to create a rife
environment for, well . . . for . . . for sniffing, smelling, sailing
with all of one's being though the ocean of, in this case, thongs,
and absorbing the object completely. I understand how you
might feel, but think about it like this—I was trying to save
YOU through your clothing. I mean, really, let's be rational
about all of this, if I wouldn't have taken the initiative to retrieve
your wet and dying clothes from their respective receptacles and

neatly placed them in plump little piles on the countertop as they awaited their turn for the dryer, then what? Truly, what would have happened to your precious little Calvin Klein's? Huh? They would have rotted, drowned in their own juices or worse, mildew. Your sexy, half-panty-half-dental-floss little gems could have developed a nasty odor and color to match, so YES, you caught me, and I'm sorry. But in essence, me sniffing your thong, OK, THONGS, was me giving mouth-to-mouth to a drowning victim. Obviously my altruism has been overlooked and all that you can see is me wearing your thong on my face, FINE, think what you want. (*Beat*) I'm sorry, I'll be leaving now. (*Realizing she is still wearing the thong on her face.*) I suppose you'll want this back. (*She hands the thong over and begins to walk away. She pauses and sniffs in the air.*) Is that Chanel or Bvlgari?

Water Re-tension

ELENA KAUFMAN

PENSIVE PENELOPE, a woman in her late 20s, confesses to her therapist.

PENELOPE: Sometimes I'm so incredibly thirsty, you know? Like I've been abandoned in the desert with only a small bottle of Perrier, a *flat* bottle of Perrier with all the fizz gone out, all *my* fizz. I say "desert" not because I'm hot or abandoned, but because I'm so parched, so dry. (*Pause*) It really doesn't matter how many liters of water I drink a day, you know? My quota of twenty-five is not nearly enough. I have five before breakfast, then I don't have to eat lunch, another ten at mid-day when it's hottest out, five at tea-time, instead of cookies or a nap, and another five in the early evening. It's a detox, a cleanse, you know, for my health. I'm washing out my colon, my liver, my inner workings, the whole thing, if you know what I mean. (*shy laugh*) It's Swami Wigamama Yogananda who turned me on to it . . . he teaches me yoga too. Have you heard of him? (*Pause*) No? I'm surprised. He's famous in California. This detox, he swears by it. Well, *he* looks good for his age. Anyway. (*deep sigh*)

(*Quietly confiding as if she's alone.*) The problem is with the water. You see, I feel like a walking water cooler. A fish tank. I imagine them swimming in my belly, gold fish, angelfish, maybe even eels. I can feel things in there, you know, plankton growing, algae gently sweeping me clean. A river courses through my innards, a waterfall escapes. Often, you know? I have to pee every five minutes, I've timed it. I've seen every toilet in this town, every single restaurant bathroom, every skanky gas station loo. (*She notices her therapist is listening intently.*) To be honest, I'll tell you they really reflect the establishment. I mean the cleanliness does. I check the charts on the back of the door, the cleaning charts, to see how many ticks there are, there

63

can be five, ten, even more. Categories are "mopping," "toilets," "sinks," "mirrors," and "refilling paper towel." My favourite resting spot is the Starbucks on College and Euclid, it's really nice in there. There are certainly a lot of ticks on their schedule, and it's bright and the air freshener is lavender, which reminds me of my grandmother's perfume. I go in . . . there for . . .senti . . . sentimental . . . (*long pause. Starts to bawl. Stops and rubs her eyes.*) Do? You? Understand? I hope you do. Do I look bloated, I mean honestly? I know I've gained weight since I last saw you. (*pause*) Yes, I have. I've put on ten pounds in the last two weeks! It's water retention. But my Swami, Swami Wigamama Yogananda, he tells me to stick with it. "You stick with it," he says. But my ankles are thickening, my belly sloshes around when I walk, my vision is blurry. I've had to change my glasses prescription! I see double . . . (*realization*) I see double. (*Starts crying again for the rest of speech.*) You see, I'm a . . .

I'm . . . (*Pause*) this is so hard.

I AM A . . .

A . . . uhh.

A . . . A Pisces. (*Short pause*) blub.

A FISH. Blub blub? (*She nods her head nervously in affirmation.*) So it should be like this, shouldn't it? Well? Shouldn't it? But still . . . still, even though I'm full up, I feel empty like I'm missing something, you know, like I'm missing my school, my community of other fish. I swam astray. Where are they? Blub blub blub! Oh! (*Pause*) Oh no! Excuse me, I have to pee again. (*she blows her nose and throws the kleenex onto the floor, exits.*)

The God of This

SHERRY KRAMER

The end of the world is perhaps a month away. Sex is perhaps the only comfort or joy left, and WILSON *is telling this story to revive her desperate friend's faith in it.*

WILSON: Last week. My last day, at my old job.

This man. I saw him, every day. And every day, I didn't see him. And every day he didn't really see me. We liked each other, a lot, that was clear. In a nice, working kind of way. But there is a way you have of seeing someone that we didn't have. Still, I liked him, and I had a really good chair that I wanted him to get first crack at.

The instant the door to my office closed behind us—every molecule of air was replaced with something else. One instant—we were just two people who liked working together—the next we were match heads someone had struck, we were Fourth of July fireworks, we were emergency flares. We tried to make small talk. About the chair. That lasted for 30 seconds. Then he said, "are you" and I said "yes." That was it. The entire transaction. And then his face—I've never seen it happen before. One minute he was a man. And the next—he was unrecognizable. Desire had rewritten every single part of his face. He had been—before—an okay-looking man, 50, 55 years old, craggy features. I think you would say he was good looking, but the change—I am not kidding and I am not exaggerating. He had transformed into a monster. An actual beast. Has that ever happened to you? Of course I have seen men—change in other ways, become luminous in front of me the instant before the first kiss, and their face blooms in front of mine, full of the next moment, I have seen that, I have seen the face, open up, suddenly smooth and suddenly, untroubled, just wholly alive, I've seen the pupils soak into the eye, and the now pour through them, and out into the whole world. But I have never seen this. I have never seen desire reveal itself with no mediation. No apologies. No reasons. No next moments. I had never seen the God of this standing before me, with nothing else in the world to do. With no other thought in his head. But *this*. And his hands—when he took me—they grabbed handfuls of me, handful after handful, my whole body, I could feel him say in actual words, could actually feel the words, each time his hands opened and closed, the language was clear, *this this this this*.

Sometimes what you feel the first instant they touch you is simple need. I like it when it's need, I like the push that needing gives to it. Sometimes it's escape he's looking for, he needs to slip out of the grasp of whatever now he's gotten himself trapped in. I like that too. Sometimes a man has been drowning—you can actually tell, as he grabs you, as he uses your body for a rope, a ladder, how long he has been under the water, how long it's been since he's taken an actual breath. And those times scare even me, but they don't stop me. A drowning man hangs on to a rope in a very special way. But the worst times are when all you hear in their hands is the word MINE. This desperate, sharp drive to make you—not you, any longer. But theirs. This passion they have to crush you into a package of now that they can fuck at their whim, as hard as they can, and then put the entire package into their pocket and take it away. Not even for use again. But so no one else can have it.

And sometimes, sometimes, sometimes—it's true, sometimes when he touches you, what you feel is love. But you can't count on love, can you? What you can count on, what you do deserve—by birth, by right, is *this this this*. It's like an endless ribbon of steel, it's like the Golden Gate Bridge, ripped off its pilings, and wrapped by those hands into armor around you, you are safe from all your fears. You do not long for life. And you do not fear death.

Excerpt from *Slither*

CARSON KREITZER

*FANNY LOU is a carny snake dancer from the 1930s. Fanny Lou
enters in a slightly shabby sequined costume with gold spangles. She
places a large boa into a wooden box, closes the lid, sits on it. Sweat.
Slowly, she sponges off the gold spangles into a basin of water.*

FANNY LOU: Get a lotta marriage proposals, this line of work.
Any kinda show business, you get a lotta dates. Snake dancers
get marriage proposals. Never one of 'em worked out. I been
brought home to Mama quite a few times. She never has liked
me yet. I don't know why the proposals. Men look at me and
they think I know something. I got some kinda knowledge
behind my eyes.

'S true. I know. Things. I know you gotta dip the snakes in
cool water before the shows in summer. Cool down their blood.
Then they're grateful, keep quiet for the show. If you don't cool
down your pythons before a summer tent show, you could definitely be dead before the dry dust settles on your sweat and
sequins. Not on purpose. They love me, as much as a snake can
love a woman. But they do get angry. Anger is a large part of
love. And they forget their own strength.

I also know this all's a damn ugly joke. Don't take that the
wrong way, I don't mean this, what I'm doing. I just mean the
whole thing is all. This isn't so bad. Beats picking fruit, which I
done since I was old enough to bend. Couldn't hardly get my
arms around the basket. Sure beats waitressing for nickels ten
hours in grease and sweat and smoke, gettin' your ass pinched
every time ya got two plates in your hand. Get a lot more respect
in my current line a work. I am treated with the reverence and
wonder they oughta feel in the presence of their own wives. It's
the same body, boys. This country'd be a whole hell of a lot

different if every woman had a snake. I don't think it's a bad idea. Put me outta work, but that's all right. I'd still have my snake.

Then maybe one a these days one a them boys would ask me home to meet Mama. She'd open the door with her ball python draped around her neck. And she'd smile at me. She'd say come on in, honey. I am so glad to meet you. She'd say you know my son here doesn't have an ounce of sense in his head. And I'd say, Yes ma'am. I plan on takin' care a him. (*Fanny Lou pulls on a kimono.*)

I don't gotta do the real sex shows too often. Mostly it's just spangles and a little sliding around. The other kind's not too bad, though. Not as bad as I thought, first time they asked me to do that kind. Snakes don't mind. They don't give a shit one way or the other, really. I will always love them for their patience. Don't care about being carried around in all that smoke and light. Noise of the yokels. Sometimes eight shows a day. They don't mind. Just want my warmth when it's cold. To be dipped in cool water when it's ugly hot. The warmth of my neck, under my hair, when it's cold.

Excerpt from *Penalty Phase*

DIANE LEFER

RENEE, a middle-aged woman, is somewhat bewildered, emptied. But when she recalls how she addressed her mother's killer in court, her natural feelings of pain and rage cross the line into frightening savagery.

RENEE: Revenge. Forgiveness. Neither one made sense. Both of them more than I could bear. So my heart went where pushed. Kill him! Closure! If I had just been a little closer, closer to kindness when the rage overcame me, I would not have been swayed.

Buell Anderson murdered my mother. He spent ten years on Death Row and I spent ten years making sure he was gonna die. I fought and fought and fought to have him put to death. That is what I did—that's ALL I did—for ten years. August 10th, just before midnight, they established the I.V., got a good saline solution drip going, connected up the three vials, at midnight, one, two, three. I got my closure. My fucking closure, that's what they call it.

There is no closure, but I'll tell you, there is satisfaction. It wasn't so much seeing him die, but you know how they get to request a last meal? He asks for two hot dogs, a bowl of chili with Tabasco, curly fries, one-liter Diet Coke—Diet?—strawberry ice cream, red vine licorice, and bubble gum. They wouldn't give him the bubble gum. I thought, man, he's gonna be pissed. The state's gonna kill him and they won't let him have a piece of bubble gum, that's just the sort of trivial bullshit that gets to that sort of scum. Killing him, that's nothing, but he can't chew bubble gum, *that* fucked up his last hours on earth, one final meaningless conspiracy of the world against him, something stupid and irrational which is the only kind of language a man like that—the sort of animal who kills a mother—that's all a beast like that can understand.

It took ten years. Ten years till they put him down. I testified at his sentencing. I got to speak right to him. "Do you understand the hatred and contempt I feel for you?" I asked. "Can you understand language, the way humans do, or are you just an animal? Do you shit where you stand? Did you grow up caged? Did your mother try to pull out your vicious teeth and nails, that you should think you could kill my mother? What do I want? I want you put to death so you'll never hurt another human being. When they give you the lethal injection, I hope they have to probe and bruise to find the vein. Do you have veins? Slack channels against which your cold blood slops and slops without a heart to push it? If they turn your tainted flesh to dog food, it will poison the dogs." I felt alive when I said that. I felt alive when they refused him his bubble gum. I felt alive when they killed him.

And now—?

Belt Loop Man

BARBARA LINDSAY

VARLA sits on a bar stool with a drink and cigarettes. She continues to drink throughout.

VARLA: He's a professorial sort, really. Bit of a belly. Kind eyes. Smart. You know. Not my type. My friend Louisa introduced us. I thought, "Whatever for?" But one doesn't like to be rude right away. So I perched for an easy escape and submitted to chat. He's got a stunning vocabulary, actually, which he employs without pomposity, although, of course, the correct use and pronunciation of "aficionado" and "acuity" hardly merit sexual reward. I was literally counting down the minutes before I could gracefully dump him and retreat when I noticed his belt had missed a loop, which for some reason I found rather idiotically sweet. That's a dreadful word to describe a man, isn't it, "sweet"? Not a man whose clothes you'll be tearing off any time soon. But he was, terribly, terribly sweet. I found myself wanting to cuddle him, hold his hand and walk through the park, lick my fingers and run them through his hair. Can you imagine? I can't. But it was enough to persuade me to go out with him for what I assumed would be an evening of either beat poetry in a coffeehouse or a chocolate soda and some heavy petting. When he arrived to pick me up the next night, I noticed immediately that his belt had once again missed a loop, a different one this time. Now, this was annoying. Right before my eyes, he turned into some sort of scarecrow person, unkempt and trashy. Anyone who's missed a belt loop twice, you expect him to have dirt under his fingernails and not much on his mind. There was no backing out at this point, but I mean, really. He barely managed to pull off the evening; in fact I wouldn't even look him in the eye until he'd said "sonorous," "epistolary," and "deciduous" and had spoken familiarly of Mombasa. I decided to give him the benefit of the doubt. Anyone who misses a belt loop twice could at the very least not be called vain. And he did seem to have some money. So he asked again, and I agreed, with a reluctance I hoped he would interpret as coy. Isn't that just me all over? Coy? All right, once more, and a dressy affair this time. And I'll be goddamned if he didn't show up at my door having missed, yes, another belt loop. Well, now I knew. Now it was plain. *He was doing this on purpose.* In a stroke, his whole scheme was revealed, clear as water. The son of a goddamned bitch was gaslighting me. He meant to drive me mad. No grown man misses *three* belt loops. That kindly smile, the erudite conversation, the tousled hair, all of it masking the black heart of a misogynist. This was too goddamned much. I was not, I repeat, *not* going to be played with this way. Who the goddamned hell did he think he is? *Three* belt loops? Not on my watch you don't, you evil, disingenuous, covertly hostile son of a bitch. So I waited. I waited until dinner. And then, right in the middle of the restaurant, right in the middle of the main course, right in the middle of a word, I turned the table over right in the middle of his lap. I've always wanted to do that. All I needed was a reason. And he gave it to me, all right. Three belt loops. My ass.

Excerpt from *The Last Seder*

JENNIFER MAISEL

MICHELLE approaches a man in Penn Station.

MICHELLE: Ummm, excuse me—hi?—look, I know you don't know me, but you look like someone who might . . . might be open to a complete stranger asking you . . . I'm not some psycho-chick, in case you're thinking I am which I'm sure you are—here's my license, so you know I'm me . . . here . . . library card, museum membership, prescription card—so at least you know I'm a semi-cultured literate insured psycho, I guess—thank you for not running away. It's just that for months I've known this was coming, there's been this impending dread which was only exacerbated by the Hallmark store across from me—its windows a mad succession of hoblins, goblins, witches, and candy accented by Happy Jewish New Year and Day of Atonement cards and Halloween wasn't even over before they added Indians and Pilgrims decorating Christmas trees sprouting out of Plymouth Rock, of which I doubt the historical accuracy, and then Valentine's day, hearts everywhere since New Year's and now they have Easter Barbie, Easter Barbie for Christ's sake, which really gets me up in arms even though I'm not religious—really, it's more of a cultural thing I have to admit, but all they'd have to do is stick a jar of gefilte fish and a Haggadah in the leftover Easter Barbie's hands and we'd make all the little girls with mezuzzahs on their Malibu dream houses very (*She catches herself in the rant*) happy. . . .

Right. Well—every day . . . every day some relative calls me to confirm whether I'm bringing flourless chocolate cake this year to seder—with my family Passover is a big hullabaloo—not so much in a do-everything-according-to-the-rules sense but more in a digging-horribly-and-obsessively-into-every-detail-of-

73

your-life-between-appetizers-and-desserts sense—and since it's the last time . . . well . . . it's all much more . . . that. But they're really not calling to find out what I'm bringing, but who I'm bringing and I couldn't put up with hearing Aunt Mabel say, "So Michelle, why don't you have a man yet?" in her frog voice. Again. I'm tired of making excuses and I'm tired of sympathetic "I've-got-a-friend"s. And this, this is the last year so it becomes important in a way I can't explain. So I'm walking up to you, and you must think I'm crazy and I know you don't know me but you're wearing a nice suit and you looked somehow . . . right . . . and that's a step in the right direction anyhow. Do you like matzah?

Sewing in Syria

ELIZABETH DAÑIEL MARQUIS

MANSOURA, a seamstress from Syria, is almost fifty years old and built like a man.

MANSOURA: Here in America, they tell you to sew forward, like a clock, but I sew this way, against the clock. I am not behind. I take my time and do it right. I be here twenty-three years, and ev'rybody ask for Me. They no carry go to American shop. They know when someone do right. When I stitch, I let myself go home. When I turn the fabric in my hands and following the patterns, the colors and shapes, I see my own patterns, I follow my own fingers. When I do hand work, always I am in Syria. When there are flowers in the fabric, I see the flowers in Syria my Mamma pick and I sew the petals like I draw a picture when I a girl. I not from Iraq. Not from Turkey. I from Syria, North of the Jordan River. East of the Mediterranean Sea. We are desert. But that does not mean we are without. When we come here, to the United States of America, our capital does not just become Washington, D.C. Our capital is also Damascus, one of the oldest in history. Here I am a citizen, yes, by paper. And sometimes by heart. But inside, God know, I remember ev'rything. And when I sew, I go home ev'ryday. I remember ev'rything. My mamma when she young and beautiful and take care me and teach me to remember, keep my faith in me. She teach me to make my own life with my hands. Not my life, I mean, God make me. (*She makes the sign of the cross.*) I make my living.

Helen

ELLEN MCLAUGHLIN

The legendary Helen has been stuck in a hotel room in Egypt for seventeen years, while a copy of her, made by the gods, has been causing all that havoc in Troy. Helen has spent her time wondering what is being done in her name and how the war is faring—she doesn't get cable—in this very free adaptation of the play by Euripides. She is finally visited by ATHENA, *who tells her just how dreadful the war was. Upon being asked by Helen, "What do the gods want from us?" she replies.*

ATHENA: You're too much, kid. You know what we love about you people? You die. And that means you've all got stories. That's why we came up with you. Even the dullest mortal life has a beginning, middle and an end. It's so fucking poignant. It could be that the whole Trojan War was just a big fat dramaturgical mistake on our parts. Way too tidy. Our desire to wrap everything up with a single enormous blow-out just ended up diluting all the stories down to one unsatisfying truncated shrug of a narrative. I mean, it's not like it's your *fault,* but we lost respect for you guys. You just looked like so many panicked beetles scrambling around on that dung hill. Or maybe it was the monotony of the deaths that got to us. Not that there wasn't a lot of *variety*—we could watch people get blown to bits by bombs, cut down like wheat by machine gun fire slicing across rows of stumbling men, or of course there were those endless agonizing deaths, all the boys lined up in their cots, oozing through their swaddling in the tent hospitals—oh, there were *variations. . . .* But really when all was said and done, it was just a whole heck of a lot of death. And it turns out that death makes human *life* interesting. But that death *itself* isn't particularly interesting. Because you all die the same way. Looking surprised.

It's amazing. Here you are the only creature on earth who knows you're going to die—it colors your entire existence from your earliest moments of consciousness. You can even spend years on a battlefield, watching *other* people die left and right of you, but when your *own* death comes, *as you always knew it would*, you're still, like, "What? ME? Surely you don't mean ME!" (*Amused*) It kills us.

Somewhere Special
(with You)

BRIGHDE MULLINS

ALLISON, 35 years old, a professor at NYU, speaks on her office phone to a man she met the night before at a Mensa Mixer; she is surrounded by books, and she is hopped up on caffeine.

ALLISON: When you mention the Greeks, Tom, I think about, may I tell you what I really think about? You just said that they were, back in the day, not afraid of saying the Wrong Thing, which I am usually slightly afraid of, you know what Emily Dickinson says: "Be careful what you say, no bird resumes its egg." That's the first line of one of her poems. Do you love her? I love her. I love Emily Dickinson. Much more than Walt Whitman, although he has some good lines too, they aren't quotable in the ways that her lines Leap To Mind, they just Leap To Mind, there I go again. I have thought in quotation marks for so long, Tom, but when you mention the Greeks I will tell you that what I think of, and I know it is not a right answer, it is not "Correct" but I think of coffee cups, those paper cups that you get at the deli, those blue cups with the white columns drawn on the sides, and the word COFFEE spelled out in those choppy, slashy Greek-style letters, and I think of how good the coffee tastes, and how much I love the taste of the coffee in a paper cup with Greek lettering, and why paper? Because the paper absorbs the acid, takes out the bitter. Sometimes, before I go to sleep at night, I hear, in very fatalistic fashion, this voice saying, "And what do you have to look forward to?"—And I think, you, I mean I, I have coffee to look forward to. (*Beat*) Tom? Are you there? Tom? You know, in certain Scandinavian countries people make little uh-huh noises on the phone so you know that they're still listening. Tom?

Verdure

LIZZIE OLESKER

Middle of the night. ASH, *a young woman, sits on the edge of the bed. Her boyfriend sleeps soundly. A red uniform dress lies crumpled on the floor, next to her work shoes.*

ASH: There are days, there are nights when I feel it. It starts here—in the chest—the middle. Not a pain, really. It's more like a break—or a crack. And like it might open up. But that it hasn't yet. Like when an egg is cracked, or a cup. It could break completely but it doesn't. A little liquid might come oozing out—a little tea leaking out onto the counter, you know? Egg white makes it stick to the box. I don't know what it is. But this one time, when I pulled my uniform off, it was wet—right in the center—six inches from the collar—something had leaked out and left a mark—a small circle—on my bra—dark—the edges jagged. I turned on the water in the sink—made it hot— cupped my hand under the faucet and leaned over. Brought water from the faucet to that place on my chest where the wet- ness was—washed it away. Looked in the mirror and thought I could see it—like this faint line—what they might call a hairline crack—barely visible—that went down the center of my body. It was black—no gray, a dull gray, like the line that shows the border of a country on a map. No blood, though—it was clean—like a small break in stone or plaster—faint, uneven— barely could see it. But it was there. I touched it and I saw that it could open up even more. That if I pushed against it that crack would deepen and that I had to be careful.

So, I lay down on the bed. On my back. Breathing. The lights of the cars moving across the ceiling. Sound of engines, tires turning on asphalt—drilling from down the road, middle of the night, it never stops. A buzz from an electric light.

Waiting for the line on my chest to disappear—that space to close up, things to dry and settle. I lifted my knees up, carefully slid my feet in, found the edge of the blanket. To cover me. (*She drinks a glass of water.*)

I remember the clay they gave us in school. It was red—smelled fresh, wet. We each had an aluminum cup with water. We were supposed to dip our finger in the water to moisten the clay. That's what we were supposed to do. Then we'd shape the clay into a bowl. Or a cat. A bunch of grapes. Or a box—a clay box made out of little rectangular slabs—even a cover with a clay handle at the top, if there was time. Once I made a coffin and then went on to make a girl to go in it. She had curls on her head that I made one by one by rolling tiny pieces of clay between my fingers and sticking them on her head with the water. My teacher came around and looked. She told me I was maudlin. Didn't know what that meant. Went home and asked but nobody there knew either. That's some kind of old word, my dad said, late that night when he came home from hauling cable. No one uses that kind of word. Weird, that's what you are, he said. (*Silence*)

But the clay. The red clay that I loved. When it had a crack, you'd just wet your finger and run it along the break. Rub along the dry line and watch the crack disappear. That's what I needed to do. The night I saw that stain. In the dark. In the sound of the traffic . . . drilling everywhere . . . new buildings coming in . . . stores . . . the lights moving . . . the endless buzz. There was water in a glass by the bed, from who knows when. So I lean over, carefully, don't want to disturb things too much—hardly breathing, trying to keep my chest still—heartbeat soft—while I dip my finger in the water. Then I run my finger along the line, the one I can see without looking, the one I can trace through some other sense. No sound. . . . The taste of that red clay in my nose, my mouth. I remember it. Want it again. The feel of it wet, muddy in my hands. Anything's possible—coffins and girls—bowls filled with fruit—ancient vessels, cups filled with tiny animals, eyes dug out with a flick of a fingernail—

then let it dry in the air and hours later, it looks like nothing. Childish. Just stupid. (*She looks to the window.*)

It's only a matter of time now for the sun to come out. For things to dry up. Cuts to close—a wound healing.

Still Blonde . . . Runs Deep

JAMIE PACHINO

MADELINE sits in a baseball cap. You cannot see her hair.

MADELINE: It started innocently enough. My mother put hydrogen peroxide on my naturally dirty blonde hair at the Maryland
shore when I was three. By junior high I had perfected a secret
concoction of salt water, lemon juice and sugar that I would apply
in specific rituals through the summer. By 16, I had discovered
Sun-In. By 18, I had to admit it. I had a problem. I had a habit.
Blonder. More blonde. Most blonde. I should have sought help
then. But with each shade paler I felt lighter, freer, flirtier. People
treated me differently. Friendlier. And by that time I was already
performing in musical theatre. Blonde! they exclaimed. Stay
blonde! In fact—Go Blonder! said more than a few.

By 24, I was nearly platinum, a sun-kissed, traffic-stopping
shade of bright golden haze on the meadow, going to the beauty
shop at least once a month for touch ups. Past my shoulders, my
salon visits were all day affairs. I didn't care. Blonde, I lusted.
Ultimate blonde—my mantra. Of course, it didn't occur to me
at the time that the only shows I could get cast in were musicals.
That men tended to over-explain car things. Or that nearly
every relationship I had started with sex, and never quite moved
to intimacy. I was striking they said. Sexy. Unforgettable. Then
they left.

I continued, undaunted. I relished whistles on the street,
dressed myself in cherry red, and favored high heels. I took a job
as a receptionist, flirted with vice presidents, and had an affair
with a married man in accounting. The transformation was
nearly complete. Okay, I kept a journal. Nobody knew. So I was
preternaturally fascinated with German philosophers and could
quote them at will. No one could guess. I wrote short stories

that actually got published. I never told a soul. I kept every appointment at the hairdresser.

The culmination of my über-blondeness was on a seven-week tour of Europe with Diana, the beautiful smoky-eyed brunette I had grown up with. Together we tore through seven countries, crossing channels and breaking hearts. Especially in Italy, where my hair alone served as an introduction to every race car driver or waiter I could ever want to meet.

And yet, as I came home with two dozen rolls of film and a truckload of memories, something didn't feel right. I looked at the pictures. French perfumiers. Greek bartenders. Scottish poets. All seemed right with the world. But then I caught one in particular. My hair looked . . . brassy . . . *obvious*. My skin seemed . . . sallow. Something was wrong. I looked like . . . a blonde wannabe. No. It must have been the light.

Then it occurred to me. I was writing too much! I had begun a play in secret and I was concentrating too hard! My hair was confused. Did I want to be a blonde, or didn't I? I put away the books and went to rehearsal. Back-to-back musicals. Performing in one, rehearsing the other.

Two months later it happened. I got cast as a wife. Not a girlfriend, not a mistress, not a saucy maid. A wife. In a straight play! What was happening to me? Okay, sure. I was a classically trained actress. Okay, right. I had done Shakespeare. But Jesus hadn't anyone heard of TYPECASTING? I had to face it. I was having a hair identity crisis.

I consulted specialists—other actresses. Well, they said, in an all night session, if you dye it back to—what was your original hair color? My God, I thought, I have no idea. Let's say you dye it light brown with a few highlights, you could go the commercial route. Young Mom, Hertz Rent-a-Car lady . . . Or! said Patrice, the Italian—you could go like a dark chestnutty brown. Get color contacts.

Play the girl next door, the virgin, the ethnic. You'd look Jewish. Could you play Jewish? Oh God, I thought. I AM Jewish. What the hell was going on?

I consulted magazines. I tried to pick out my hair on other women. Did I look like that, I wondered, looking at the natural blondes in the Revlon ads? Or did I look like the horrible roots and bad highlighting gracing the Dep hair gel ads?

I ripped out pages, tacking them on walls, surrounding myself with women. As many shades as I could find, from Cleopatra black to Jean Harlow white, trying to decipher the personality of the models, simply by the color of their hair.

Did I trust the brunettes more? Yes! I did. Did I think the blondes were sexier? Yes! I did that too! I had to face it. I was a color-ist. I judged people by the color of their hair. Therapy was needed. Color therapy.

Julie, I cried, racing to the hairdresser's. You must help me! My inside and my outside don't match! I have no idea who I am. What do you want? she asked. DYE MY HAIR! I screamed, all out of proportion. No, she said. . . . What. Do. You. Want? I looked at her terrified. She nodded. It was time to decide. You see—I had so liked being so completely blonde on the outside and so—brunette on the inside. The blonde who could discuss Nietzsche and Byzantine History, the brunette who might dance Fosse and sing Gershwin. That was drama. Couldn't I be that? No, Julie said solemnly. Choose. But I *liked* the idea that men approached me thinking I was altogether different. I *liked* the looks on their faces when they figured it out. Okay *they* got confused, but that wasn't my problem, was it? Listen, said Julie. That's all over now. Isn't it . . . ? Can't I . . . ? No, she said. Pick. And walked away.

I sat in that chair a long time.

People really do take you at your hair color. Casting directors *say* they're open minded and impartial, but—well . . . really. Men *say* they like smart women, but—not in their blondes, not when you get right down to it. Okay maybe I had something to do with it. Maybe I played blonder with certain men. Maybe I giggled a little at certain auditions. Maybe I *had* some complicity in the whole affair. After all, I was the one with the hydrogen peroxide bottle. Wasn't I? And yet. Here it was. My D-Day.

I ran through my magazines in my head and tried to decide: blonde . . . brunette, blonde . . . brunette . . . I pictured each casting director I knew: wife . . . mistress, wife . . . mistress . . . I weighed. I considered. I pondered. I delved. I thought long and hard. (*Takes off baseball cap.*) And dyed it red.

And now NO ONE knows what to make of me. But my fiancé likes it a lot. He thinks of me as one complete person, inside and out. I'm a produced playwright now. A published author. On the other hand, I recently started thinking about a few blonde highlights. Just for the summer . . .

The Strawberry Monologue

TALIA PURA

A girl, in her 20s, goes to a church for her daily confession.

Forgive me Father, for I have sinned. It has been twenty-two and a half hours since my last confession, so here I am, to unburden myself and receive absolution for my sins. I usually go to St. Michael's, over on Fourth and Grover, but Father Andrew insisted that I come and pay you a visit today. I told him yesterday, I said, see you tomorrow, or actually, you'll hear me tomorrow, I said, he he he, and he said, well he said, why don't you go over to our Lady of Perpetual Solace and Hope and give Father Matthew an earful tomorrow. I hear he's very lonely over there, he said. Well, I said, in that case, I said, I'll do that Father. So, here I am.

Anyway, yesterday after I left the church, that was St. Michael's, not your own lovely edifice, which I am sure I could grow to like, too. They say that if you've seen one confessional booth, you've seen them all, but I disagree. Yours is nice, but I am rather partial to the cherry wood in St. Michael's, even though I am sure that this oak is all fine and good, once you get used to it. And that is a very nice stained glass window you have in the nave, even though I am used to seeing one that is a little bigger and a little fancier in the nave of St. Michael's. Forgive me Father, I don't mean to be critical of your church. I hope that you won't take it personally, but the holy water, Father, for my taste, always looks a little nicer in something that sits a little higher off the floor and isn't quite so close to the front door. It just doesn't catch the light at all when I walk by. As I was telling Father Andrew just yesterday, I said, well, I said, I always gulp back a tear every time I enter St. Michael's, the holy water is in such a lovely location. The light always seems to hit it just right, no matter what time of day I come in, I said.

So, anyway, after I left St. Michael's church yesterday, I went to the market to pick up a few things. They have such nice produce and the staff is so helpful and courteous. As I was telling my mother the other day, Mamma, I said, I am so impressed with how helpful and courteous the staff is, I said. And she said, oh, she said, I've always noticed that too, she said. When you were a little girl, they always gave you a lollipop, every time we went in, she said. Well, I said, of course I remember that, too, Mamma. I have an excellent memory, you know. Yes, indeed, I said, I will most certainly be a customer for life. Unless they change their policy of being helpful and courteous. That could happen if they changed ownership. Do you have any idea who owns it, Father? Father? Are you there, Father? Oh, he he he, for a moment there, I thought you'd left, but I can still hear you breathing.

So, as I was saying, Father, yesterday, I went to the market for milk and bread. Momma asked for whole milk. I've told her a thousand times that she ought to be switching to skim milk, or at least 2%. Mamma, I said, Mamma, you are not doing your arteries any favor with all that fat. Not that she is doing her weight any favor, either. If you must know, she has a serious weight problem. But it wouldn't be kind to tell her that and I don't want to add to the list of sins that I have to go to confession for every day, so I just stick with the arteries.

So there I was in the market, right smack dab in the middle of the produce department, when I found just the nicest, juiciest, red strawberries that you ever did see. So I said to myself, oh, I said, I really should pick up some of these strawberries for Mamma's ice cream after dinner tonight, I said. I don't think that it's a good idea that she eats ice cream for dessert every night, but since she is eating it anyway, she may as well have some nice strawberries to go with it, don't you think?

So I picked up what I thought was the best looking little basket of strawberries, but just as I was about to put it into my cart, I noticed that there was one berry, near the bottom, that was actually starting to turn mushy. Well, you know that if you take home one mushy berry in a basket of good ones, it starts affecting all the other berries and before you know it, you can just forget about having those berries on your ice cream, thank you very much. So I dug down the side of the basket and picked out the mushy berry and changed it for a really good berry from another basket. (*Beat*) Nobody saw me do it, except God. I felt so bad, but what could I do? The deed was done. If I would have switched them back, one of the helpful and courteous staff members might have come over and started asking questions. I practically ran to the nearest checkout counter and paid for the strawberries, my cheeks burning with shame. I'm surprised the cashier didn't notice me blushing. She was just as courteous as she always is. Have a nice day, she said, just like she always does.

Thank heaven you were here today to take my confession. I couldn't have held it in another minute.

Moonshine

ERIN M. PUSHMAN

MADELYN, a twenty-something Atlanta lawyer, returns to her Smokey Mountain home.

MADELYN: There's somethin' 'bout runnin' through the city in the dark. Some nights, I'll run at midnight. Then when I give up on layin' in bed and not sleepin', I get up again before dawn and run more. It never makes me tired. I run until this burnin' feelin' in my middle goes away. Sometimes it won't go away, and I have to stop because my feet hurt. So then I walk. It's so dark in some places, down in the streets of the neighborhoods. Sometimes street lamps are burned out or hidden in the trees. And the lights in the houses are off. And the city's quiet. It's just my breath and my footsteps stirring up dirt and leaves on the sidewalk. Sometimes I wear my white jacket and my white running shoes. And I never pull my hair back, so the wind takes it all 'round my face, in the dark, in the quiet. And I wonder if this is how ghosts feel. There is somethin' 'bout moving through the shadows, praying for spaces without much light, runnin' hard while cities sleep.

Tricky

NINA RAPI

A party in a club. BLUE *is urgently passing through the audience, as if escaping a nightmare. She's just seen her ex totally unexpectedly and is freaked out.*

BLUE: Fucking hell. Jesus. What. Is. Going. On. What does she think she's doing? Yeah, right, no fucking way, mate. Finito la musica, passato la fiesta. You know what I mean? (*Looks toward the entrance. Shouts at "Jasmin."*) You've got to stay LOCKED IN. Do you hear me? (*Back to the audience.*) If you hear her shout, don't go there. Please. She has to stay locked in. For a while at least. There's a good reason. It's my sanity, ok? So. Stay here. Promise me? Thank you. Thank you very much. I just want to get a grip on things, tell you what happened, you then decide whose side you're on. Because we all take sides, don't we, whether we admit it or not, whether we keep silent or not, especially when we keep silent, you know what I mean? Sure. Right. Let me calm down and I'll tell you the story. (*Fast walking on the spot and taking deep breaths. Calms herself enough.*)

Me and Jasmin well. . . . It was Big, it was Mega, it was The Real Thing. I never knew anything like it. What can I say. Ace. We were up there, way up for six whole months. . . . She is dead cute . . . baby face . . . almond-shaped eyes . . . her tongue in all the right places . . . tight little arse. . . . The way she had of anticipating my every need and making sure it got satisfied. Phew. . . . Made me feel fucking A. (*Beat*) But then a few problems cropped up. You know, the usual. Like, she wanted us to do everything together. And I mean, *everything* . . . including going to the toilet! Made her feel all warm and safe, she said. So, there we were pisssssssing, together. You can imagine. . . . Yeah. And she had all these rules, like:

90

Never swallow food before you chew it seven times &
Never finish eating before me.
Never answer the phone after nine &
Never call your friends when you're with me.
Never boil eggs for more than 66 seconds &
Never peel apples when you serve them to me.

Yeah . . . So, if I made a mistake, she'd sulk. For hours. If you haven't seen Jasmin sulk, you don't know what SULK means, I'm telling you.

So . . . I started wanting some breathing space, you know? She said "Fine, I understand." But then she got into the habit of following me around. Like, I'd go for a drink with my mates and suddenly there she was. . . . "I was just passing by," she'd say. It. Got. A bit. Much. (*Pause*) I was heading for the way out fast but "please, don't leave me," she said. (*Beat*) I did love her. I fucking did love her. So I decided to sort things out. So. We arranged to meet in neutral territory, being fair and all that. We chose the Freedom Bar in Soho. So. We arranged to meet at seven and I was there dead on time. I got us a nice spot by the window, got myself a Stella and waited. And waited and waited. . . . It came eight o'clock and still no sign of Jasmin. I began to worry. Now, I knew Jasmin had a problem with time, she often lost sense of it but one hour and in a public place that was pushing it. I was beginning to see red but decided I'd better wait. "Something might have happened to her," I thought, "or maybe she is testing my commitment." She liked doing that. "Testing."

So . . . I was lost in my thoughts and this girl comes over and says: "Do you mind if I join you?" Just like that. "Why be rude?" I thought. So. "Of course," I said. There were three chairs there anyway. Besides I was getting anxious and needed a distraction. We started talking and laughing. She had a baby face too, so she felt kind of familiar. We really hit it off. But it was all innocent. Honest. At one point we were literally rolling in laughter. Just then Jasmin arrived. (*Beat*) Love! What a fucking joke. Love! Ha. A little caress will cost you seven lashes, whipping you into submission, that's love. I need it, I need *her* like a bullet in the head. . . . A mistake, that's all it was at the bar. Or maybe just a slip-up, a blindspot. A little thoughtless, I admit, perhaps even insensitive, ok. But I never meant to hurt her. (*Pause*)

She left me that night. She turned on her heels and left. And for three whole months she treated me like I was worth shit. Froze me out completely. Didn't even give me a chance to explain. (*Beat*) That hurt. Badly. Never thought she could be such a cruel, callous bitch. I couldn't fathom out how she wanted to be with me 24/7 one minute and didn't care whether I was dead or alive the next. That really cut me up. Deeper than anything before or since. And what's worse, I was on my knees begging, I was crawling in the gutter and *she was loving it!*

(*Gets cocky.*) Then I saw her at the Candy bar and I thought, "Fuck this. I'll do the ignoring this time." It was hard but I did it. She couldn't take it. Started following me around. I'd be propping up the bar, turn my head, there she was, staring. I'd go upstairs, hide in the crowd, turn my head, there she was, staring. I'd go to the basement, hide behind the speakers, turn my head, there she was, staring. In the end I gave in. . . . It was the eyes . . . couldn't resist those eyes . . . so I let her get closer . . . and closer. . . . We danced around each other for a while . . . started touching ever so slightly. . . . Then more . . . and more . . . then we started kissing. . . . The heat was on. I'm telling you. We nearly did it there and then. Phew! (*Excited*) So. We got back together . . . in love all over again. Up Up, in Heaven Again. Way Up . . . For a while . . .

(*Gets moody.*) But, see. Something had cracked, something that couldn't be mended. I couldn't trust her again. "Close up. Clam up, girl," I thought. "It's the only way. Don't let her get close and hurt you again." But the more I cut off, the more of me she wanted. And the most of me she wanted, the more I cut off. "Don't cut me out, please," she kept saying. On and on. "I can't take it." "Don't freeze me out, Blue, please. I can't take it." (*Pause*) So, I left her . . . since she couldn't take it. (*Pauses for effect, then gets excited.*) I felt so high, I can't tell you. High as a kite. I felt free at last. Free from a noose around my neck. Like I got myself back. Like I could breathe again.

But then the doubts started. "I left her out in the cold. So what? She's sulking. Let her sulk. She's hurting. Mustn't hurt." I rang her once or twice . . . well a few times actually. I sent her tapes with her favorite music. I sent her flowers, presents. I even got some musician friends to serenade her, yes even that! Did she melt? Did she fuck! She called it harassment! Bloody cheek. (*Beat. Amazed.*) She took a banning order against me. A banning order! OK, she got the law on her side. OK, she banned my physical presence from her premises. But how, yeah, how can you ban feelings eh?

(*Triumphant*) She apologized of course. Lifted the order. Realized her mistake in asking the law to sort out our problems. . . . *She's* been begging *me* for days now to sort things out and get back together. (*Long pause*) No fucking way! I'm not getting back with her! I'm a free agent now. No more pulling and pushing, thank you very much. My life's back on track, I don't need any more baby-faced tyrants to fuck it all up again. Nope. I'm strong, I'm together, I'm happy. I've "seen the light." I told her. *Keep away.* From me, my friends, my turf. This is my turf. So, I came in here thinking, "Great. This is a Jasmin Free Zone, I can relax here." So, I said "hi" to a few familiar faces at the bar and then I went to the toilet . . . you know the small one on the side.

Well, this is what happened: the door is closed and I wait. I get a knot in my stomach for no reason whatsoever. I try to ignore it. I wait a little more, then the door opens. And who do I see? Jasmin! She fucking followed me here! I stand there for a few seconds like Medusa has cast her spell on me and turned me to stone. Jasmin smiles her Mona Lisa smile. "Hi," she says. I recover instantly. I push her back into the toilet, grab the key from the inside, pull the door shut again and LOCK HER IN. Then I run down here. You know the rest . . .

(*Pause*) Now, my friends. What would you do in my place? (*Waits for some answers.*) I'm serious. What would you do? (*Waits.*) If I open that door, we're back together, I know it . . . I can't do this again. This going around in circles. I can't. (*Thinks.*) Strange she hasn't shouted to be unlocked. . . . Not that she's the type to shout, mind you. . . . . Silent and devious is *her* modus operandi. She's probably sitting there *sulking* . . . fuck . . . I mean Jasmin sulking is no laughing matter . . . shit . . . I can feel it in my bones. . . . . She's sitting there waiting for me . . . needing me. . . . .She *is* very needy. Very. Can't do a thing without me. (*She's hooked.*) Maybe I should go and see how she's doing. (*Beat*) I mean, she's LOVELY really. (*Decides.*) Yeah, that's what I'll do. I'll go and open that door.

Three Words

JACQUELYN REINGOLD

A woman in her early 20s talks to herself or to the audience.

I can't believe it. I can't believe this is happening. "I'm sorry, I have bad news—not good." I can't believe it. We left the office. We couldn't find a cab. We ate chicken with cashew nuts. We drank lemon lime seltzer. We rented *Broadway Danny Rose*. We went to sleep. We woke up this morning. We went to the hospital. Three Words. A.M.L. He had a cold. It was a cold. He went to the doctor. We ate Italian food. We joked. We said we want a plateful of fried platelets, please. Because his were falling. I didn't even know what they were. But his were falling. Platelet. One, a microscopic disk occurring in the blood. Two, an important aid in coagulation. A rash on his ankles. I said it's heat rash. Tiny drops of blood below the surface. Not enough platelets, you get blood. His doctor leaves this on a piece of paper in his room and walks away. He starts to cry. I start to cry. A nurse pulls me into a supply room with red garbage bags, and she's six-two, and she gives me a paper cup of orange juice that tastes like grapefruit juice, and she says with a big smile don't cry in front of him, he shouldn't see you cry, he should see you helpful and positive. I want to say hey, wait a minute I can't even believe this. He's my sweetie, I just moved into his apartment. I was spackling. I was filling in the cracks and the places where it won't go smooth. I bought ten gallons of hint of peach, and now I have to leave him here to get chemotherapy, whatever that is, because he had a cold and a rash? What I want to know is who's going to paint the apartment? I'm supposed to leave him here with people who have staples in their heads, and liquids pouring out of them, and no tongues, and no hair? I'm supposed to believe he's one of them? He can't be. I know he can't be. But I

95

don't say anything, and she asks me if I'm feeling better, and I drink the juice. We go back to his room. She says have you been to a sperm bank? We don't know what she's talking about. Didn't the doctor tell you? No, he didn't, so she gets us a pass. We leave through the front door. We can't get a cab, so we walk, and we start to laugh because shouldn't you not be wandering around New York with a deadly disease? What if we got on a plane and left? Maybe it would go away. We get there. He fills out a form. It says "diagnosis." He asks me how to spell it. L-e-u-k-e-m-i-a. He says, I'm sorry this is happening to you. We go into a brightly lit cubicle. There is a table, a chair, a stack of *Playboy*s, and a box of tissues. I take off my shirt. I help him come, being careful to get it all in the cup. . . . Those are our children. I want them. I want us to have those children. Don't let him die. I'm supposed to call his friends. I should call his friends. I have to tell his friends. I'm sorry, I have bad news—not good. I'll say it over and over. He's sick. He needs your help. He's in the hospital, he's getting chemotherapy, he has A.M.L. Acute Myeloid Leukemia. Then I'll go to bed. In the morning I'll take the bus. I'll bring him the newspaper and a whole wheat bagel.

Song of My Sister

MOLLY RICE

A geeky fourteen-year-old GIRL *is looking through her collection of Manga comics.*

GIRL: Yeah, she's weird, I guess, my sister. I think maybe she's part elven. Oh no, there are people like that—on the Internet there's whole groups of half-elven and elven people. I think she is. And not just because of how she looks. There are other things.

Like food. A lot of the books I've read, they'll tell you elves eat, like, mushrooms and leaves and stuff like that. But the really old stories say all they need is water and sunlight, kinda like plants. That's how it is with my sister, I think. 'Cause she doesn't eat food. I'm not sure what she's made of, but I'm pretty sure it's not the same thing as what's in you or me. Her body doesn't go by our laws, I don't think. It just doesn't.

All the girls at school are in like awe of her, you know, 'cause she doesn't need to eat and she's so skinny but yet she's so strong and so tall. She's really beautiful. I read on the Internet that elves are like, on average, six foot three and weigh one hundred and fifty pounds. My sister weighs a lot less than that, but she is six feet tall. She could be a model. But she doesn't care about things like that.

I have tried to be like that. I've even tried to not eat. But it doesn't stick with me. I'm too addicted to being mortal, I guess. I'm full of human and I know it, where she's human plus—something else. Magic. You can't change something like that.

You can learn about it, though. I spy on her. In the mornings when the alarm goes off I lay there and watch her get ready. She doesn't know I'm watching her, though, because I've mastered breathing like a sleeping person and seeing through slit

97

eyes. She takes a long time to get ready, but most of that time she doesn't do anything but look in the mirror. She stands in her underwear facing the mirror and stares straight at herself. Frowning. Concentrating, like. Then she raises her arms and looks at herself. (*She does this.*) Then she turns sideways and looks at herself that way. (*She does this.*) She pinches the little bottom part of her stomach that just barely pooches out, even though there's nothing there, just skin. (*She does this.*) Then she turns to face the mirror again. She does it this way every time. (*She demonstrates. It looks like a strange slow dance.*) Over and over. It's so amazing. Like she's doing a spell. She's, like, storing up all her magic for the day ahead. Her face is so somber, like she's praying almost.

But that's nothing. You should see her at school. She is like this—this *arrow*, shooting in slow motion through the hall. Straight and perfect and—unstoppable. All this noise is happening around her—all these people talking and shouting and laughing and being stupid. And there's that funky smell of people all around. And all the noises and smells are jagged and fuzzy like static on a stupid human radio. But she shoots through them all, clear as glass, clear as a bell. No smell. No sound. Like it was all a cheap cloth, a thin, falling-apart fabric of some old dress or something, and she is a needle pushed through by some secret force all her own. Everything dissolves around her. Nothing can stop her. Not words. Not me. Not my mother. Nothing.

Happy

TANIA RICHARD

KAREN, a thirty-four-year-old woman, is having dinner with a friend who just announced her engagement.

KAREN: I'm happy for you. I am. Regardless of what my face looked like, or what I may have said, *inside*, I was doing cartwheels, flip flops, so much so, I could puke. Well, puke in a good way. Puke for joy, so to speak. I was just surprised. Not surprised that it happened. You deserve it, really. I was just surprised that yet another one of my friends is on their way to that life we're all supposed to be having . . . and . . . WOW! I was just surprised that there was going to be one less of me. You know, "the gang." The "singles gang" of which I am fast becoming its only member. But that's not your problem. Not anymore, anyway. 'Cause, YOU, are on your way! I am happy for you! I am. It's just uh . . . can I be honest? I think I'm getting a little scared. Like really, really scared. TERRIFIED! Because I'm beginning to believe that there isn't anybody out there. Like nooooooobody. And I'm really pissed at all those adults who sold us that bill of goods when we were young. Ya know, grade school, high school, college, marriage, kids. Nobody ever mentioned that you might end up alone. They left that part out. Didn't they? Maybe if I had known. (*Shouting*) But here I am, and here I sit, and except for an occasional dinner with a friend— I! Am! Alone! And the silence is deafening! And my heart is heavy! (*Beat*) But I really am happy for you. I am.

True

ROBIN ROTHSTEIN

CASSIE, a woman in her 30s, speaks to a very close friend.

CASSIE: So. I'm walking home Wednesday night after seeing *Frankie and Johnny in The Claire de Lune.* Walking up Ninth Avenue, thinking about all the surgeons I'd seen over the course of the past two days, the jumble of voices and information swirling through my head. The hard, fucking unfair decisions I'm being forced to make. (*Pause*) When I have this realization. (*Pause*) This was meant to happen to me. No wait listen, let me—during the play, there's this part where Johnny asks Frankie to drop her robe because he wants to revel in the beauty of her nakedness? (*Pause*) And there they are. Two, perfect, full, natural, beautiful breasts. And Johnny just stares at them in total wonderment and awe. He's so overcome by their beauty, he can't find enough words to describe how sublime they are. (*Pause*) Right then I feel this sting in my heart, and hear this voice in my head say, "No one's ever going to say anything like that to me now." Anyway, it's after the show, and I'm walking down Forty-fourth Street towards Ninth Avenue, and I'm thinking about my breast, and how it will change, and how I will change, and I'm freaking out about all this as I'm walking up Ninth Avenue— my breast, the play, Frankie's breasts, all the doctors, all the words—all these images flashing and intertwining in my brain. (*Pause*) But as I continue my walk up Ninth Avenue . . . out of nowhere . . . this moment of clarity pierces its way through all the noise in my head. And I start to realize . . . this unforeseen tragedy that's befallen me? It's actually a gift. It's an opportunity for me to discover how tough I am. To realize the potential I have. The strength I have. The will I have. And now, I'm feeling really good! And . . . and I start thinking about you . . . and seeing you tonight . . . and I'm feeling all charged and my footsteps are landing squarely on the sidewalk, and I'm noticing all around me how life is so beautifully choreographed and alive, and how *I'm* feeling so alive. And something is telling me that I'm *supposed* to be aware of all of this stuff at this very moment for some reason, how everything feels so connected and true. And I'm almost home, and I'm imagining myself telling you about all this tonight . . . when I notice this figure up ahead. And all of a sudden, I'm jolted into this kind of . . . crazy reality. You know, like when time seems to stretch for a few long dream-like seconds? (*Pause*) I believe and don't believe who I see walking down Ninth Avenue at 10:40 P.M. between Fifty-third and Fifty-fourth Street. (*Pause*) It's you Alex. It's *you!* You don't notice me, though you easily could if you just glanced my way, but you don't. Anyway I'm all bundled and it's dark, so it's unlikely you'd recognize me if you did. I feel my voice rise in my throat to say "hello," but before I can, I get this sensation, like someone putting a hand on my shoulder, suggesting to me not to reveal myself to you at this moment. So my voice stops in my throat, and I just . . . let myself be a witness to this very . . . miraculous experience, knowing at this moment, that I am totally in sync with something much larger than I will ever understand. I feel like an angel, watching you as you stare straight ahead, deep in your own thoughts, as you float down Ninth Avenue. (*Pause*) I could've walked up Eighth Avenue. I could've stayed in the theater longer, or left faster. But I didn't. I walked up Ninth Avenue, in one of the largest cities in the world, with all these particular thoughts about my life, including thoughts of you, and then, there you were, a daydream I willed into solid form. I know you don't believe in those sorts of things, but that's what it felt like. You should've been wearing a hat by the way. It was too cold that night for you not to be wearing a hat. (*Pause*) Anyway . . . what I'm trying to say . . . I've always lived my life . . . trying to achieve what I'd like to be true, instead of just dealing in the moment with what actually *is* true, and acting on *that*. Most of us don't live in our own truth. But

I did on Wednesday night. And it felt unbelievably good. I know I'm going to be okay. I don't know how. I don't know why. I just know. And I also know . . . that I love you Alex. I love you very much.

Small

LOUISE ROZETT

A woman is at dinner with her boyfriend.

I'm sorry—this—No, no, no, no. Wait. I'm not sorry. This isn't going to work. I'm looking for a man with a small penis. I'm not kidding. I'm not even trying to be mean. That's what I want. Guys with big penises are, generally speaking, arrogant, and suffering from "better than" syndrome, which you obviously are. Even while I'm sitting right here in front of you, in ridiculous underwear that I bought for your benefit—which is going up my ass, by the way—you're looking around to see who else you can have, who's "better than" me. There's a woman behind me, to my left, who seems to be much more interesting to you than anything I'm saying. (*She looks over her left shoulder.*) Sure, she's pretty. I can see why you'd find her attractive enough to justify making me feel insignificant. Now, guys with small penises, on the other hand, are not looking at other women over their dates' shoulders. It wouldn't occur to them to do so because they're so grateful that they found women who will stay with them despite their small penises that they wouldn't do anything so obvious and stupid to damage their relationships.

I'm not particularly proud of this. But the world of men has been analyzing me physically since I hit puberty, which was around 10, lucky me. And I know my flaws, physical and otherwise, because I've been seeing myself through men's eyes for almost as long as I can remember and apparently, I am not anything to get excited about unless I'm naked and begging for sex. What I'm saying is, I learned very quickly to rely on male attention for self-esteem, and though I've been trying to change that for years, quite frankly, it's not going anywhere. I don't like it, but fuck it. Fuck it! And if that's the case, then the last thing I need is to be involved with some guy who can't see that I'm doing everything I can to be attractive to him because he's checking out other women while we're out to dinner. So I'm insecure, and maybe a little crazy, but that's me, and I've just decided I will not embark on another relationship with a big penis.

Excerpt from *The Clean House*

SARAH RUHL

MATHILDA is a Brazilian woman in her late 20s. She cleans house for a woman doctor.

MATHILDA: The story of my parents is this. It was said that my father was the funniest man in his village. He did not marry until he was sixty-three because he did not want to marry a woman who was not funny. He said he would wait until he met his match in wit. And then one day he met my mother. He used to say: your mother—and he would take a long pause—is funnier than I am. We have never been apart since the day we met, because I always wanted to know the next joke. My mother and father did not look into each other's eyes. They laughed like hyenas. Even when they made love they laughed like hyenas. My mother was old for a mother. She said it took time for a woman to develop a sense of humor. She refused many proposals. It would kill her, she said, to have to spend her days laughing at jokes that were not funny. (*Pause*)

I wear black because I am in mourning. My mother died last year. She died laughing. Have you ever heard the expression "I almost died laughing"? Well that's what she did. The doctors couldn't explain it. They argued, they said she choked on her own spit, but they don't really know. She was laughing at one of my father's jokes. A joke he took one year to make up, for the anniversary of their marriage. When my mother died laughing, my father shot himself. And so I came here, to clean this house.

How Darlene Coleman Became a Professional Eulogist and the Most Popular Girl on the Funeral Circuit

KRISTAN RYAN

DARLENE COLEMAN, 40s–50s, impeccably dressed in a cheap royal blue suit and cheesy high heels, stands at a podium holding a wad of papers, speaking to funeral goers. She looks around the audience briefly and begins speaking as if she is wrapping up a funeral service.

DARLENE: Since we are about wrapped up, I want to thank you all for coming to pay your respects this afternoon to Miss Elsie Beasley who has passed on to that glorious world awaiting those of us who have lived a good and decent life. As you know, food will be served in the social hall immediately afterwards, so I'll make this last bit quick. The funeral director, Mr. Hermes Wilson, has voiced to me some concerns a few of you have had about the length of my eulogy for a woman some of you have so unkindly referred to as a moldy old backbiting shithead, but let me say you've misjudged Elsie Beasley as I have so frequently pointed out during my testimony to her life. Yes, that's correct. Few of you knew what a kind heart she had. So let me say, one more time, that when you all accused her, back last Christmas, of replacing the ground coffee over at Shaneequa's Home Girl Café with chewing tobacco ON PURPOSE you were MIS-TAKEN. Elsie Beasley accidentally used that container of tobacco she was planning on taking over to Mr. Wilson's sister, Venus, who was living in the nursing home on East 11th Street and who was dying for a smoke. . . . Miss Beasley wanted me to make sure everyone who got sicker than a dog on laxatives . . . her words, not mine . . . that what happened was an ACCI-DENT, pure and simple, because those cans looked exactly alike to her, and as you know, her vision was known to go in and out. She also wanted me to tell you that she never married, not because she was a bitch on wheels as so many of you have called her in those anonymous letters you sent her over the years, but because she was a virgin and wished to remain so for the love of God Almighty. (*Pause*)

The first eulogy I gave was at the Gladys County Funeral Home for my next door neighbor, Mr. Virgil Wiley. He was a foul old man, mean as a wart hog, who spit on the sidewalk in front of you just to see you slip, and who I once caught peeping through my keyhole. I only went to his funeral to make sure the bugger was really dead, so it was as big a surprise to me as it was to everyone else that I rushed to his aid, accidentally launching my career as a professional eulogist in the process. (*Pause*) Mean as he was, it seemed a pity to me the man's own blood hadn't given much thought to him . . . so I got to thinking how pitiful life can be in the end for some folks and wondering if this was going to be the shortest funeral on record, when all of a sudden the minister asked if anyone could remember a kindness Mr. Wiley had shown in his lifetime. I almost laughed out loud when I heard that because I was still steaming over old man Wiley stealing my laundry and tossing it into an alley. I looked out my window one afternoon and what did my eyes behold but a child riding by on a tricycle wearing two pair of my panties on his head and my best bra thrown around his neck like a fancy scarf. Naturally, the sight of that child with my under-things sent me into a hissy fit of enormous proportions. But even with that memory so fresh in my mind, the minister's words set me to thinking and damned if I wasn't struck with the thought that maybe that old man had been misunderstood, even though it was unlikely. But what if he had been? My mama always said there are times when a person can't trust her own eyes. Take me, for instance. I lost my job as cashier over at the Food Lion because Miss Never-Been-Married-Never-Even-Turned-a-Head Myrna Tuttle said as God was her witness I had been helping myself to peaches for some time, but I called her a liar as loud and as many times as I possibly could before the police came and escorted me home. (*Pause*)

So there I was at Virgil Wiley's service KNOWING what it is to be wronged when I got so overcome with divine inspiration I jumped up to that minister's podium and screeched, "I KNOW A KINDNESS, A BIG ONE," and I proceeded to share how happy Mr. Wiley had been as a child to see his little sister born and how he cared for her his whole life until that night she jumped into the James River grieving over catching her sweetheart in a love knot with a bald man with one gimpy arm. (*Pause*) After I had had my say his daughter wailed like a lost child. The couple with the eight screaming brats and the super left with bloodshot eyes, swollen noses, and snot-filled hankies. (*Pause*)

Miss Campbell, hunched over with her head hanging like her job was searching the pavement raced up to me and said that in her ninety years in the neighborhood she hadn't known Virgil Wiley to do one nice thing, that if there was a devil it surely was Virgil, but when she heard my eloquent speech about how he had loved his sister and how no one had truly understood who the real Virgil was, that she, being ninety-two and most likely one breath away from death herself and surrounded by great-grandchildren who thought of her as nothing more than a smelly old shitbag, why she knew I had a gift and was compelled to confess her sin of attending funerals for the food and the free flowers right then and there. Before I can express my amazement, this tiny prune-faced woman whips out a fifty-dollar bill and a piece of paper with her name and address on it and makes me promise to write a eulogy that will make . . . and I'm quoting her here again, "those money-grubbing asswipe relatives of mine see how wrong they were about Miss Eloise Campbell." Then she tells me that if I can write up a piece about her that sounds as truthful as that pack of lies I just told about Virgil, she'll tell all the old folks she knows about my special gift and she'll make sure that in her will there's another two-hundred dollars for me for showing up and giving her final eulogy. But I say, "No, you pay me the money up front because, honey, you could drop any second now." Miss Campbell says okay and then tells me she can die in peace now knowing that some do-gooder who doesn't know shit from shinola won't be talking stink about her life . . . her words again, by the way, and opens her patent-leather purse crammed with money and hands me another two-hundred, pumps my hand and totters off. (*Pause*)

As a paid eulogist, my biggest selling point is my ability to make people BELIEVE that YOU, THE WICKED, filled with hate and discontent in life, were actually the sweetest, most thoughtful people who ever lived and that even though your relatives wouldn't feed a starving vulture your guts, when I am finished delivering the eulogy you paid for in advance, you'll find yourself staring up from the fires of hell only to see folks in a heap on the floor crying their hearts out over losing the one person they once thought had the blackest heart in history. Remember, I am the one who will add that flash of perfection and glamour to the life you never had. It's my words that will make those waiting at the bank to pick up your last dollar sorry they never knew the true you, the you I will have carved and shaped in their minds with a flick of my wrist and a quick snapping of my tongue. So, go ahead, grab one of my cards and pick up that phone when you get home and give me a jingle. Now that I don't work at the Food Lion anymore my social calendar is as wide open as the peach bin was on the day they let me go.

Miss Wonderling's History Class

FRANCESCA SANDERS

MISS WONDERLING, a sturdy teacher perhaps thirty-four years old, stands erect, holding a pointer in front of her class. She speaks with a British accent.

MISS WONDERLING: World War One. (*Beat*) Every day the witnesses to this war are dying. The people who remember the blood, the sacrifices, all it entailed. (*Dramatically*) The war with its trail of evil. . . . Pay attention, students. Pay attention as we examine what led us down the evil garden path to fight . . . man against man. (*She notices a student coming in late.*) Don't dally, Miss Warbridge. Take your seat. (*Beat*) Now where was I? Oh yes. With World War One we often ask ourselves . . . Miss Kandeline, if you don't remove your shoe from your ear, I'll be forced to send you to the principal's office. Do I make myself clear? (*Beat*) Good. Thank you.

Yes. The war to end all wars was a classic example. . . . (*Turning her head to look at Miss Epstein.*) Miss Epstein, would you kindly remove your hand from Miss Warwick's face? (*Beat*) I don't care if she said she was looking a bit pasty this morning, that's her problem. Besides as you undoubtedly know, slapping her won't help. It's the pinching of the cheeks that brings the rosy color to the face. Now as I was saying . . . (*Sing-song*) What is it, Miss Webster? (*Beat*) Can you be excused? For what, pray tell? (*Pretends to be listening intently.*) No dear, it can't be your time of the month so soon. Remember? It wasn't two weeks ago you said the very same thing and went off for the afternoon with . . . what was that chap's name? Oh yes, Teddy. Two weeks! No one is that irregular. (*Annoyed*) Please put your hand down,

Miss Webster. I say, put it down. I don't want to hear another word about your biological abnormalities. (*Beat*) No, Miss Webster. I actually don't believe you're . . . no I'm not calling you a freak. Merely a scientific anomaly perhaps.

Back to Winston Churchill. When he was a young man he . . . What is it now, Miss Blumberg? (*Beat*) Well, you had your hand up, forgive me for calling on you. (*Beat*) Oh really? Well that's fascinating, Miss Blumberg. (*Beat*) Believe it or not, yes. Yes, I do feel World War One has a place in history. (*Beat*) No, I actually don't think of it as the dark ages, though I suppose to someone as young as yourself . . . No I was not calling you immature . . . I was merely pointing out that to someone with your myopic slice of life. . . . (*Beat*) I say, Miss Blumberg, you've been studying your vocabulary. Yes, I suppose that was a bit of a slam. In any event, World War One is not only studied, as you put it, in this sleazy girl's school, it's actually being studied throughout the UK and I daresay, in several other countries as well. (*Beat*) No, I don't have proof. (*Beat*) No, I can't name them all but . . . yes, I suppose that would make my comments myopic in nature. Thank you for pointing out my shortcomings, Miss Blumberg.

As I was saying, Winston Churchill began talks regarding . . . yes, Miss Mills? No I don't think I attacked Miss Blumberg's character. (*Beat*) No, I most assuredly do not think it's caused her permanent damage. In any case, it's too soon to tell. (*Beat*) No, I don't think I'm being flippant. No, I don't think I'm being flippant at all. (*Beat*) No, I haven't singled her out for my target practice, as you say. I merely pointed out that . . . what's that, Miss Mills? No, I wasn't in love with Winston Churchill. He was quite a bit older than I, I'm afraid. (*Beat*) Yes, it is hard to believe anyone can be older than I, but I'm afraid Winston was. (*Beat*) No, calling him by his first name is not a term of endearment. (*Beat*) He was a historic figure and I think . . . what's that, Miss Mills, you never heard of him before today? Well, I daresay your reputation for not having high level reading skills must be warranted. (*Beat*) No, Miss Mills, that wasn't slander. Slander is when you say things that are untrue about someone and repeat it in a public forum. Instead, this is. . . . (*Beat*) Well, I'm sure you're right, Miss Mills. I'm sure Winston Churchill never has appeared in his own music video but then neither has Tony Blair and . . . no, not the Tony Blair that works in the Lancaster Pub. This would be a different Tony Blair altogether, Miss Mills. Different altogether.

Perhaps we should be studying current events. (*Beat*) Ah, this you know something about? I'm thrilled to hear it, Miss Mills. Could you relate a current event? I don't dare ask if you know a current event that might relate directly to World War One. I don't dare. So, Miss Mills, you have the class's attention. You can name any current event you like and speak for one minute on the topic. I'll time you starting now. (*Pause for about ten seconds.*) That was fascinating, Miss Mills. Anything else? (*Beat*) No really, it was fascinating. I simply had no idea that Michael Jackson was peculiar. (*Beat*) Yes, indeed! That's exactly the kind of insight I was looking for, Miss Mills. Exactly! Does anyone have anything to add to Miss Mills's clever observations about historical current events? Yes, Miss Potash? (*Beat*) Yes, I believe he does have a skin condition, Miss Potash. (*Beat*) Yes, that is sad. Terribly sad. Yes, he has had quite a bit of bad luck. Now if we can move on. . . . No, Miss Webster, I haven't forgotten about your medical emergency. I am quite able to go to my maker knowing I've prevented you from going to the bathroom. (*Beat*) Yes, I do like to live dangerously. Now class if you'll turn to page forty-seven. . . . (*At the end of her rope in a British way.*) What is it, Miss Nettelton? I suppose you'd like to discuss movies or perhaps music videos. Perhaps you'd like to extol the virtues of Michael Jackson and condemn me for not taking Miss Webster's forays into the school corridors seriously. (*Trying to listen.*) Please speak up, Miss Nettelton. What was that you say? (*Beat*) Yes, thank you, Miss Nettelton. It probably is he. (*Beat*) Yes, Winston Churchill most probably is the chubby guy on your grandfather's mantel.

The Artist of Transparency

LISA SCHLESINGER

A pair of old men's boots on stage. The sole of one boot is torn so that it flaps like a mouth. A girl, late 20s, enters barefoot. She wears a roll of duct tape on her wrist. The actor may use the boot as the mother or address it when she talks to the window washer.

There are too many pigs on the highway today. Their flat black eyes peer through the vents in the steel trailer trucks. You can sense the terror and misery in their one-eyed gazes. They don't know what they are, where they are or why, but they know they are trapped. I fly past them, thinking how lucky I am not to be a pig, thinking they are eyeing my freedom with longing, if they are capable of longing for something they never knew. Interstate 80. Swear to god, it can kill you. People getting on, getting off, speeding past, heading towards, getting away, the road ragers, the cell phoners, the highway righteous, the gun law reformers and their get a gun signs. It's crossed my mind to shoot those signs. Travelers are lonely people. We go back and forth and take it all in, yellow field, blue night, and remember things.

My mother. Used to leave her cigarette burning in the ashtray while she folded the road map ever so carefully and tucked it into the glove compartment. She was a goddess of quiet and tidy. I'm lying in the way way back of our blue Dodge Dart wagon and I stare up at the sky. She says *hey, you know what this is?* It's sky, a silo, and a big red barn. *No,* she says. *This is where the airport is going to be.* Why do we need an airport? I ask. *So people can fly. I flew once,* she says. And I see her up there, a blue bird, hovering, but maybe it is just the smoke off her cigarette, ascending.

Years later I see the window washer in that airport. With one arm he sweeps a long arc up the left side of the glass across the top and down. With the right arm he returns to wipe the water away. I know he's an artist of transparency because I never saw a window that way before. It's so clear that outside I can see the ghosts of the barn and silo. The man behind me says *Doris, you don't have to be the first one on the plane. You get on the plane and you suck in the jet fumes.* The husband is huge, red, and explosive. *Doris, I'm telling you, it's not going to make the plane leave any sooner.* Doris is prematurely aged. She laughs. The children stammer. The older one puts her arm on the suitcase, the younger one slaps it off. Looking around, you think there's some kind of malady affecting the human race. I stare hard at that window washer and he turns around.

The Dodge Dart stalls in the field of trusses and girders. *You know,* my mother says, *I was Miss Iowa in 1969. I just wanted to get out of my little house on my little street of my little town and that was my one way out as far as I could tell. I didn't want to be Miss America. I wanted to drive straight across I80—Illinois, Ohio, Pennsylvania, New Jersey, through the Lincoln Tunnel—you know the Lincoln Tunnel—you drive in one state and come out in another state altogether. I'd go in Miss Iowa and come out Someone Else. They crown me at the state fair and I am standing here, waving, looking at everyone looking at me. We're all just display. The horses, pigs, the cows, the bunnies, and me. When the contest is over there are only two choices: slaughter or breeding.*

I'm pretty lucky. I look normal on the outside. It's a great cover. Two eyes. A pair of knees. One ass. No hint of what kind of questions I might ask you if you hang around long enough. At this point the window washer notices my normality and he takes interest. *Can I help you?* he says. You live around here? I ask. I hope not. It's too noisy. The way I see it the world should be just enough. I don't mean moderate. I mean it shouldn't kill you with things. The noise should be like music not like cargo engines. Things should taste like what they are—like strawberries, not like strawberry gum, you know what I mean? *No, I don't live around here,* he says. *I live here. An airport is like a city. You can eat here. You can get almost anything you want. People come and people go.* Right off I know this is my guy. I can see us in his city. We're the only two people left, wandering the halls, settling in. To be sure I only have to ask him one question: You want to go for a drive? (*To audience*) Don't look at me that way. You know exactly what he says. He puts that squeegee and rag in the bucket and we're gone.

It's a summer evening and my mother takes me out to see the first plane take off from our airport. She says, *women hate to be alone, it's ridiculous, someone should change that.* She gets into it behind the stage at the State fair with one of the judges. He's an artist flown in from New York City, he does a portrait of her with one line of a pencil and she says, *yes, that's exactly what I would be if I were just one line.* He gives her the drawing and another line something like *I want to look at you for the rest of my life.* But now he's got to think about it first because what would being with her do to his art? Meanwhile, she loses the title because she's fucking the judge behind the stage at the State fair and guess what he gives her: a ten. And she's pregnant to boot. You can see where this is going. It's going towards me.

The window washer and I get together and we make something new, something that never was before. It lasts about 12 hours. We are on the road, off the road, back on the road, on the side of the road. We are moving, not moving, paused at lights. We try things out we never tried before, over the back seat, in the well, in the way way back, under stars, the white moon, in a field of alfalfa. What changes is the inside of the vehicle with the sweat of us all over it. What changes is the view out the window to the world. What changes is time. He says, *I want to look at you for the rest of my life.* What I want is love that parts its mouth. You don't know if you're going towards it or it's pulling you in but then you are so far in you don't know who is who.

My mother parks by the runway and we watch the planes take off and land. She says *I loved your daddy and he loved me too. I think. Honey, if you ask a man are you in or out, the honest one says both. The liar says, I do. Your daddy said let me think about that and he went out for a drive. He's out there just driving along thinking about love and art and things when at the 189th mile marker, just outside Newton, a truck full of pigs breaks away from its rig, flips over and kills him. Dead. I guess he got his answer. One day I had him and one day I didn't and it's hard to believe a person could go that way.*

I've got to pee. That's how it is. When I'm nervous my stomach growls. When I love hard I've got to pee. I pull over at the first rest stop. Can I wear your boots a minute? The window washer gets out of the car in his sock feet, comes around to my side, opens the door for me, kneels down in front of me and puts his boots on my feet. *You've changed me,* he says. *I didn't know I would change. I'm in a whole new state.* What do you think I am, I say, The Lincoln Tunnel? But he doesn't get it because he's never been out of Iowa. The thing is he's making me nervous, down there on his knees. I can already see the aisle, the forks, the knives and the china. *You're like,* he pauses, *really talented.* When a person says *like* it means the exactness has gone out of things. I got it from my mother, I say. *But you know what, girl? You want too much. People like you get in trouble. Or they get pregnant.* I got that from my mother, too. *I would've liked to meet your mother.* Would've? I ask. *A person shouldn't want too much. A strawberry only wants to be a strawberry. It doesn't want to be a plum.* What about a pig? I say. *A pig just wants to be a pig.* I want to know you, I say. He stands. He stretches his long armed window washing body slowly towards the sky. Everything that ascends eventually disappears.

My mother takes me into the supermarket on her birthday. She lifts me into the shopping cart—not the part with the little leg holes—the part for the groceries. She pushes the cart up and down the meat aisle. *Baby girl,* she says, *this is the only aisle I am ever going to walk. Here. Beef. Chicken. Lamb. But pork chops! But bacon!* She shakes her fists at the freezer section. *Guts guts guts.* (Beat) *The thing about your birthday, baby girl, is you appeared. The thing about my birthday is I've got to give myself something.* She gives me a balloon. *You wait right here.* I see her through the dirty plate glass window like she's walking through clouds. I watch her disappear into the parking lot. She drives out to the airport field that is now an airport, minus the silo, minus the big red barn. She takes the first plane. She ascends. Going going gone.

I step out of the restroom and into the parking lot. The window washer has left me his boots but he's taken my mother's car. He's used the Band-Aid method. It's more painful but it's fast. I pray a little to the highway gods and the prayer sounds like this: How do you decide who gets ripped off quick and who gets smashed by pigs and who gets left to walk? And anyway, god, fuck him. I know those pigs long for more than that damn pig truck. Even the window washer wants more. Even Doris' husband has that longing.

(*She tears off pieces of duct tape and tapes up the sole of the boot, laces them tight. Stands.*) When a person leaves you they leave a space inside you the same shape as the one they took up. The window washer left a clear pane to see through. What I see is a whole world. And my mother up there in flight. (*She opens her arms up in praise.*) It's a beautiful morning for a walk. (*She walks.*)

Too Cool

LAURA SHAMAS

Loud techno bar music. Laughter. MIRANDA, *an elegantly dressed young woman of 33, wears a cocktail dress and holds a glass of wine.*

MIRANDA: Now that it's so cool to be a lesbian, it's ruined the dating scene. Oh, yeah. Everyone is doing it and if you haven't done it, you act like you did or would have if you'd been younger in the 90s or at the very LEAST you dated someone who was bi before you got married. (*Miranda dances a bit to the music, then stops.*) Everyone loves gay women and everyone wants to have one lesbian friend or better yet a lesbian couple with baby in their inner circle. Face it. You are not cool unless you have us in your lives. Straight men want to be able to fantasize about the fit gay gal pal making it with their wives. Straight women want to be able to man-bash and express their real intellectual thoughts with us without fear. We are in demand. We are needed. Like doctors and shrinks. We keep society purring. And it's more stressful now than ever before.

But the hardest thing that this cool status has done is make it tough to weed out the pretenders. You know what I'm talking about. Once something gets cool, then you get all the opportunistic wannabes, the unschooled imitators, the "I'm exploring my sexuality" dingbats. I say, pick a lane, for God's sake. How hard can it be to know your own libido or at least be on a first name basis with it? Do you really want to tell people you're a faux lesbian? It's tough now even in a place like this (*Indicating her surroundings*) because you can't exactly walk up to someone and say: "Are you at this dyke bar for the glamour or for real?" No. Not a classy way to start a relationship.

I have a friend who met her last girlfriend through a chat room. I think it was "Gay and Lesbian Chat Room Seven" on

AOL, but it could have been "Big Beautiful Women Three." Whatever. She swears it works. But every time I try it, I get the same lousy response. You go into a chat room, and the first thing that happens is someone with a ridiculous screen name—something like IMADYKE69 or LICKME4REAL—IMs you with (*said like a question*) "Age/Sex/Location?" Then "Any Naked Photos?" Right. Bingo. You know it's a pathetic teenage guy, trying to fool lesbians, hoping to get orgiastic pictures of groups of women for his own disgusting purposes. That is so MALE. As if asking about your age, gender and where you live is such SCINTILLATING and ENGROSSING conversation that you will immediately send a nude picture of yourself to a complete stranger. Yeah, that's all it takes to get to see us naked. We are so desperate. NOT.

And these teenage boys think they are fooling people. If you ask them for their photo, to call their lesbian bluff, so to speak, they send you one of the many pitiful airbrushed girly photos they've acquired through other channels. I believe the proper name for it is Internet Porn. Just what I want on my computer—a bunch of naked drugged-up women with breast implants. I mean, what is happening to our society when TEENAGE BOYS sit around at keyboards pretending to be gay women? Yeah, I know they are trying to be cool, too, like all the rest of you, but what is happening to the world when young men usurp the act of defining what it means to be a dyke? I mean, looking back at the history of the world, haven't they usurped enough without trying to horn in on the lesbian experience as well? Is nothing sacred? Is it too much to ask that lesbian chat rooms be for lesbians?

Jessie

S. M. SHEPHARD-MASSAT

JESSIE speaks to her Aunt-in-law, Beverly Ann, after returning from her husband's funeral.

JESSIE: Beautiful service, but in the middle or near the end, I drifted. Kerry Frank's death is still sittin' on top of my head, has not traveled downward thru' my neck, lung cavity, into my heart. Is not chokin' me, or stiffenin' my fingers or toes, or makin' steam rise from my armpits. It is a beautiful spring day, innit? I could remember bein' younger an' readin' the head-stones; bein' struck by the dates: BORN thus 'n so. DIED this 'n so. Real people under the grass. Kerry Frank used to take me wit' 'im to straighten off his parents' graves. Now, he's lyin' there next to them. Mama Opal, Papa Evan, a son an' a little baby granddaughter. I used to wonder wha' the world would be like without 'im in it. Would the birds stop callin'? Would the earth quit? Goin' 'round on its axis? Would some great event change life as we knew it fo' everyone? At once? At the moment he passed from existence? In commemoration of? Well, he was a good person, a great person an' none a' these things happened so, wha' the heck? It was a beautiful day anyway. Only thing. He's dead. My Kerry Frank. The Lord giveth the gift. They say Satan takes it away. (*Cradles invisible baby in her arms.*) Jus' like when I found out my baby girl was so sick. When I got right down on my knees. Holdin' my sweet baby close to me. Even before my eyes could well up I prayed, Lord God Almighty. Please don' take my baby. Not my chile. Not my gift. Not the gift you gave to me special. But, my sweet girl didn' live, did she? (*Drops her arms.*) Six months old an' she didn' live. Aunt Bev, I meant to beat the devil down this time, tho'. I swear I did. I meant to kill 'im wit' all my heavenly might, but it didn't matter if I'd pulled Kerry Frank 'roun' on a chain to keep 'im clean, did it? Him wit' tha' big, ole job he had. Was goin' so many places wit' it. Yeah, he went plenty places. I pushed him thru' the doe' a' every church ministry, camp meetin' an' prayer vigil in Georgia, Alabama, both Carolinas an' Tennessee tryin' to get them spirits off 'im but you can't make people stay when they wanna go. You know tha'. They make themselves airborn, don' they? (*Spread her arms, twirls reaching skyward.*) I believe they do. I believe they lift themselves right on up toward the clouds lookin' just in one, upward direction because they are no longer after the earthbound for the answer, because they already know. I believe tha'. I believe.

Hollywood is Calling

LYDIA STRYK

A woman of indeterminate age stands alone. She does not speak for some time. She shivers, impressed.

As the blind prophet, Jorge Luis Borges, once said, "Like all women and men, I was given bad times in which to live." Mind you, the truth is. And I hate to admit it. (*A pause, she struggles.*) But here goes. I'm letting myself in for it. (*She sighs, readies herself.*) I had a happy childhood. There. It's out. Go glassy-eyed. Smile condescendingly. Your disinterest bordering on disgust. I'm used to it.

Have I not failed the great litmus test of all martyrs? Around the dinner table with my best friends. A litany of woes and outrages. Each story topping the last. Abuse, neglect, discrimination, poverty. And then there's me. Yes, my childhood was wildly happy. Setting in motion a youth of contentment and inner stability. I know, I know, it borders on obscenity. I have floated on a charm. Bathed in love. Corn fed. Strong limbs pushing towards the light. Like a fucking sunflower. That I end up here, is it any wonder? In these bad times in which to live.

Borges also remarked, that despite the worst, fear is meaningless. As is hope. Because they always refer to future events. "Events that will not happen to us, who are the minutely detailed present." Don't you love that? No fear, no hope. No future, no past. So, I don't know how long I've been standing here. Or better put, here I am! (*A pause, she gasps a little breath.*)

Last night I dreamed of a steak. I was cutting through it, slicing open its steaming flesh, bit by bit. But was that me dreaming? Or the steak? Was it, perhaps, the steak dreaming of being eaten. Seared and peppered. Was the steak dreaming me?

I wasn't always alone out here. There was once a man I wanted forever. Like Borges said, "I was standing on my corner, feeling eternity," when he joined in. Right here, next to me. I never knew his name. He was a practitioner of Falun Gong—aligned to the principles of Truth and Compassion. He sat in peaceful meditation, and he said, "Sit by my side." Falun Gong is an ancient practice for improving the body, mind and spirit. Thousands have been beaten and tortured, imprisoned without recourse to trial or justice. Disappeared and murdered . . . He sat here, black hair, jeweled onyx in the sun. Then he was gone.

You're wondering what I am doing here. I am not waiting for a bus. It's cold. It's always colder when you're standing still. But then, you go inside your body. You are inside your body, working. I'm my liver sloshing around, my heart pumping away. I'm my lungs whooshing, my stomach churning. . . .

I stopped carrying signs. No War. Stop the Killing. Feed the Planet. Save the Children. I stopped shouting slogans and singing, "We Shall Overcome." I stopped marching, I stopped joining. I stopped. Stopped still. And my protest. It just grew and grew! No words left to contain the suffering. I started. Standing. I stand. Stand still on the planet. Feel the inside of my body, but also outside it. Underneath it. I don't feel my feet. I feel the planet spinning me. Yes. I am dizzy with it. And the boiling core pushing up to keep me warm. (*Pause, gasps a little breath.*)

Do you remember the watermelon's cool sweetness? Crisp-breaking on the tongue?

Tell me what enrages you? Hauls you under with despair? I will carry it for you on my silent protest. The extinction of the leather-back turtle? (*She pauses in silent protest.*) Or the disappeared peoples of the earth? Imprisoned in dungeons? Dropped from airplanes in rice sacks? I carry the pain of leaves turning. Red, orange, brilliant mauve. The tears of rivers choking on the spume. I take the slights, slaps, yearnings, rejections. Transborder, transgender. Daily and seasonal tragedies. They all reach me. And along with the anguish, I carry the rage. A rage so loud it shuts out all sound.

Borges said, "If you suffer starvation, you will suffer all the starvation there has been or will be." (*She takes a breath, appears unable to continue, she sits, slowly, cross-legged.*)

So I stopped eating. I no longer remember when.

Did the strawberry's juice dribble down your chin? Red like blood? (*She is silent.*)

36146 and Juanice

SHANESSA SWEENEY

JUANICE, a 24 or 25-year-old black woman, sits on her porch in a lawn chair. She has a pack of cigarettes in her lap, an ashtray on the ground to the left of her, and a less-than-half-filled bottle of Hennessy, a bottle of Budweiser, and an empty glass on the ground to the right of her. She puffs on her cigarette.

JUANICE: Square? (*Offers cigarette.*)

This yo' first time 'round these parts of the country? Yeah, you can tell . . . don't too many folk come 'round here and when they do, you know they from outta town. You down here 'cause of that news report, huh? Yeah, they say it's a least fifty-seven percent that got it. And that even countin' the ones that ain't been down there to get checked. Ain't no telling fa-real, 'cause folk 'round here don't like to tell they bizniss, they might tell somebody else's, but they sho ain't gon' tell they own, 'specially if they out doin' dirt. Fifty-seven percent? That's a lotta folk to be walkin' around with that Ninja. Fifty-seven percent?! So that mean, if a hundred people live here in this one zip code area, like they say in that report, then fifty-seven of 'em walkin' around with HIV. (*Continuously puffing on her square.*) Guess that's why you down here, huh? Guess that's why you talkin' to me . . . I don't know where it come from, righteously . . . I gotta guess, but I ain't fa' sho. I don't ask no questions, hell, I figure, I ain't got no right. I ain't no saint myself ya know. Besides when you layed up with yo' man, the last thang you thinkin' about is a damn question. 'Specially if he tellin' you he love you. And when you young, dumb and full of cum, that's all you wanna know; is that yo' man love you and he layin' that pipe right. Hell, I figure if the answer don't come to me by the good Lord, then I don't need to know. . . . (*Starts putting out square.*) But I got three boys, and they need to know, ya know? My babies . . . they all I got—they ain't like me though. And they ain't gon' be like me either, I makes sho'a that. They better than me. . . .

(*Lights another square.*) They say these'll kill ya . . . child, these my best friends. They never give up on you. Yo' friends might forget aboutcha, yo' family might forgetcha, even God give up on ya sometimes, but these. . . . (*Shakes her head.*) Uh-uh. Hell, I figure I'm gon' die anyway, right? (*Takes another puff.*)

Well, I gotta go and get my boys from school . . . rain, sleet or snow, I makes sho I'm up at that school everyday when that bell rang so we can all walk home together—it's the little stuff like that that matter, ya know? Maybe you can come over befo' you leave . . . have dinner or somethin'. . . . Well, you got my number. . . . (*Stands.*) Well, you have fun walkin' around here in AIDSville . . . you got one down, now you got fifty-six mo' to go. (*Leaves.*)

The Gamester

FREYDA THOMAS

A woman of "a certain age" who gives young men money in exchange for favors. This is an original scene added to The Gamester *by Regnard.*

MME. SECURITÉ:
A maid, 'twixt twelve and twenty, ought to be
The soul of innocence and purity.
Näive, exuberant, a budding rose,
So pliant in the hands of eager beaux.
She whispers, "Teach me how to do my duty."
Of course it is essential she have beauty.
The next ten years, the lady must be sure
To cultivate a slightly ripe allure.
She knows the way, but hasn't learned it all,
In case some afternoon you chance to call
While hubby's safely sheltered at his club,
She'll learn a few new things—ay, there's the rub!
From thirty till she's forty she must be
Endowed with wit and personality.
She shines in the salon, she sparkles plenty,
Convinces you that she's but one and twenty.
She laughs and quips, a true comedienne,
She's talked about by women and by men,
Yet both seek out her charming company,
A fascinating sorceress is she.
Yet when she is alone, and forty plus,
And all those people cease to make a fuss,
She looks into the glass, and tiny fears
Creep up like lines that steal away her years.
Sweet youth beyond her grasp. She sighs and cries,

Not quite content that age will make her wise,
Yet wise she must become, what can she do?
One look into the glass says she is through,
Her wit and beauty gone in one bright flash.
Oh, if she lives past fifty? She needs cash.

Excerpt from
Ajax (por nobody)

ALICE TUAN

ANNETTE and her friend Alma sit in a makeshift steam room, waiting for their sex dates to arrive.

ANNETTE: God, I'm all red. Have we had enough steam? (*Pause*) Hah Alma? (*Pause*) Alma? OK, I'm turning it off cuz I'm too red. (*Hissing stops. Steam slowly clears.*) Jesse won't like that. The red. Is it OK if I go with Jesse? I have this thing for dark eyes, because . . . well I have dark eyes and . . . the other guy, what was his name? Alan, I think it's Alan, right, he's got these really piercing blue eyes and, well to tell you the truth, I can't . . . I have a problem with guys with blue eyes because . . . did I tell you this story? Alma? Did I? Yoo hoo, are you there? I mean the other guy Alan is really cute, I mean almost too cute, I mean well I think, I mean you have blue eyes and he has blue eyes and, maybe you guys see eye to eye, I mean, I didn't mean it like that, I think you can have a lot of fun with him . . . it's just that when I was in high school, I had this mad crush on this guy with blue eyes and . . . I mean it was a mad crush, I'd have violated my people to be with him I mean, I'd have peeled off my skin and sewn it into lampshades myself if he wanted, I mean it was really awful how mad I was for him and . . . he told me he couldn't be with me because I could never give him a blue-eyed child because dark eyes always take over light eyes since the light eye gene was *always* recessive and wouldn't show up. . . . I mean he said it nicely and all, but. . . . So I kind of have this problem with blue-eyed people I mean it kind of, it kind of crushes me . . . especially cuz we could have changed the colors, I mean they do have those colored lenses . . . but I didn't think to say that. So if they're blue-eyed and we're having fun, they have to keep their eyes shut.

AHHHHH! GOD! I hate ants I hate ants I hate ants! Look at them they're so desperate and they all swarm for like some stupid small crumb of stale nothing. They're so, I mean they're just all over it like that one morsel was the greatest thing that ever happened in their lives. GOD! I hate ants I hate ants I hate ants. I'm burying them in Ajax. Here, crawl through this, motherfuckers. Crawl! Crawl! (*Sweetly*) A little sprinklette of water . . . and now you'll all turn blue. I'm so happy to wash them down the sink and turn on the disposal. KKKKRKKRKKRKKRRRR. It gives me great satisfaction to know they're KKKKKRRRRK chopped up in the disposal. KKKKKRKKKKKRKKK. That's why KKKKRKK I just laugh and laugh and KKKRRRK and laugh. HA HA HA HA HA HA HAKKKKKRRRR Clean and crushed. HA HA HA Clean and crushed. Ha ha haKRKRRKKha KRRRRK ha ha KRRRRK ha. Gone. Back to normal.

Excerpt from *Rotten State*

KATHRYN WALAT

ELEANOR lies on the couch.

ELEANOR: Alive or—dead? It's a yes-or-no, green-or-blue question. A or B—to be or . . . not—I've got a 50-50 chance of getting it right. But the problem comes when I want to argue with the teacher. When I tell her that true-or-false doesn't work for me, because in movies I laugh during the sex scenes. Because I like my cereal soggy and crunchy at the same time—I always choose none of the above.

The problem is, sometimes you feel like a nut, sometimes you don't. So I choose sleep. And I don't mean metaphorically, like sleep equals death—like, we love Fido, but let's put him to sleep. And I don't mean simile, either, even though I keep saying like. I mean sleep like, why not do this on the couch all day instead of looking shit in the eye? I am fond of prone. Of recline and zone. Of curling up, blowing off, dozing, drooling, waking up and telling the time by the lineup on TV.

But there is the waking. And that's a bitch. It feels incredible for seven seconds—until you remember whatever it is you went to sleep to avoid.

I know five different ways that I could kill myself without even having to leave this room. One: Cocktail of nail polish remover. Two: Exacto knife in wall socket. Three: Mother's little helpers. Four: Daddy's razor. Five: Bang! I find that list as comforting as farting in the bathtub. Of course my ex-shrink would say it's a "crutch" because I don't "deal well with change." Because even if I knew it would be sweet mama paradise, it would still involve something other than this couch and the lovely swirly patterns in the plaster of this ceiling. And what if they don't have VCRs? Or Almond Joys. And the problem is, we don't know.

(*A knock at the door.*) So my all-American firearm stays under this cushion, a pea for my princess ass. I open my eyes. Get up. And go look to see what's behind door number one.

Widow's Walk

BARBARA WIECHMANN

RUTHIE, an old woman close to dying, lies in bed staring out. In her fever she believes that her late husband was actually a sea captain in the nineteenth century and she the "widow" that waited for him. She speaks to her son Robert.

RUTHIE: Oh, when your father comes. Smell of sweat and whale blubber. Smell of fish on all his fingers. Home home your father is—Harry home with all his heartiness the fevers and sniffles— "You'll catch the death of cold you idiot! Off off with your boots—" Muck ridden boots covered in slime. Horrible. (*Beat*) That was from being inside the whale—the first time he died. (*Beat*) I'll tell you about your father! You know nothing about your father! How many times your father died while I stomped up and down the widow's walk. While I waited how many times he died. NO. NO. You know nothing! Three times he died. While I waited. First time was the whale. Whale ate him. Snapped him up during a squall. Swallowed him live and wriggling. Days later they brung him to me. Dead. Blue and dead they brung him. Stretched him flat and bloody on the new carpet and this is what he said: "Cut me out of the belly, Ruthie. The boys, bless 'em, harpooned the brute and sliced me out. Cut from the belly bloody into this world, born again by God's design, plucked out by heaven itself for nothing but adventure and escape. Now what did you do Ruthie?" . . . (*Beat*) What could I say? So he gives me a little squeeze and two weeks later pop he's off again and up I go; creak up them damn stairs in my starchy frock, up to the roof to wait for the second time. (*Beat*) Sea siren. Little slut sucked the life outa him down in her sea castle. That's the truth. Body washed up all bloated. Some neighbor kid found him and give him back to me. What could

I do? Brung him in, cleaned him up, gave him some cocoa and a piece of ass and next I know pop he's off again and up I go, creak up them damned stairs, up up to the roof, face all clouds, lightning in my hair—the neighbors thought I was a witch. (*Beat*) Who cares anyway. What did I have to do but wait around for the next time? The last one. Last time he died was the storm. Taken by a wave. Gave up his life ta save the crew. Just like him eh? The bold act, 'eh? When the ship was sinking and the lifeboats was all fulled up he lashed himself ta the mast. Oh yes, the last of the boats was gone and the big wave come an he'd tied himself to the mast, strapped himself to it so he could take the storm dead on, look at it straight, face his damned fear, go down with the ship, drown like nobility, die like a hero, and every man would hail him an every woman dream of his image but me—round and round the widow's walk in my black and face all clouds screeching "who the hell cares how you go if you go it's all the same ain't it? Who the hell cares! Selfish dreams of bravery. COWARD!" (*Pause*) I don't make things up. *I'm* not the one. (*Beat*) You know I don't believe. Don't believe in sea stories. Shitty stories. Sea worms and mermaids. Bazooms out ta here. I never saw a mermaid. Men are liars. All that shit about hair and big bazooms. I never saw a mermaid. They just say all that to make the rest of us who aren't mermaids feel crappy.

Love Juice, Excerpt from *Dating and Mating in Modern Times*

ELIZABETH WONG

ARLENE, 40s, dressed in a stylish tailored business suit, devilishly enjoys a private secret she's about to share. As if to offer a congratulatory toast, she holds up a glass beaker.

ARLENE: Here it is. Happiness in a glass. The average male in his lifetime will ejaculate 30 to 50 quarts of this stuff, containing 350 to 500 billion sperm. Wanna taste? Just kidding. Mostly, it's fructose, that's the main ingredient in sperm, fructose. (*Aside*) Of course, I haven't swallowed since 1980, ever since the advent of AIDS and well, the calories. One squirt has about five calories per teaspoon. (*Beat*) I've got about—(*Looks into the beaker, swirls it around*) six teaspoons in here, that's a lot of love juice. Some guy must have spent some pretty productive quality time with *Hustler* or *Playboy* or some porno on DVD. My O.B.G.Y.N. says the average ejaculate is about one teaspoon. Average speed of ejaculation is 25 miles per hour. I like knowing stuff like that. If we're playing the game Trivial Pursuit, you want Arlene the ace kick-ass trivia queen on your team. (*Sniffs inside the glass.*) Smells nice. (*Checks her watch.*) It's got a shelf life though, so. (*Examines the beaker like it was fine wine.*) I'm due to ovulate any second now. I wanted to get acquainted with these little guys before we get down to business. They brought in the frozen sperm, sat it on the table to breathe like a fine Bordeaux, warm up to room temperature, wake up those little hibernatin' sleepyheads.

(*To the glass.*) Go little guys go! Gotta give these frantic wiggly fellas plenty of encouragement, considering everything they have to do, ricocheting off the walls inside me, on a crazy head-banging search mission to penetrate one of my ancient eggs. Average swimming speed 4 millimeters per second. (*Checks watch again.*) Once the doctor gets here, he's a real wiseass, always kidding around, we get along grrrreat. And he's really considerate, he warms his hands up, *and* he warms the speculum, that plastic medieval torture clamp. Open wide, wider. That's more action than my vagina has seen in eons. The doc always rolls his eyes, laughs no matter what, that dear man. Oh, so I'll climb onto the table, saddle up in the stirrups, and well, you know. This is sooooooo exciting.

(*Holds up the beaker.*) This stuff in here, this beaker of love juice, it's really . . . (*whispers*) special. This is not just jack juice from some poor college student trying to pay his tuition. Uh huh. (*Peers into audience.*) I see you out there. Or some perverted sicko who wants to spread his seed and propagate the planet with his offspring. This sperm is genius ejaculate. Smart cum. Some Nobel Prize-winning scientist got happy, and put all his genetic code into this glass beaker. Yeah, I know. I know it sounds like some freaky master race Aryan obsession. But look, if I'm going to have a baby all alone, with no guy in the picture, then I'm not going to get knocked up by some anonymous DUMB sperm. I want smart sperm. I want a *smart* baby who will change the world, use their brilliance and brains to find the cure for the common cold or help the blind to see. I want an Ein*stein* or a Bern*stein*. A baby to heal the world, with ideas, with poetry, with music. Everything in this glass beaker comes from an IQ over 200. Yup yup yup yup. The other sperm banks and fertility clinics only list race, age, medical histories, favorite hobbies. Who cares if you like stamp collecting, bungee jumping or internet porn? Give me sperm that can calculate the square root of infinity. This cryo-bank is the only one around keeping track of IQ, education and profession. Of course, you are taking them at their word. They say this is *Nobel laureate*, but it could very well be the *booby prize*. Remember in the news, that big fat sloppy doctor inseminating all his patients with his own doctor balding/man breast/beer belly sperm? Yes, it's all a leap of faith. Of course, my doc looks like he stepped out of the pages of *Esquire Magazine*, so if he did that, oh yeah baby, what a baby! What am I talking! I should just be grateful I can try for a baby at my age. At my age. (*Beat*) It's amazing really, and well, kinda sad, that modern technology is making guys obsolete. Men are making themselves irrelevant with their brave new world. I came from a single parent household, I thought I'd never do this without a man in my life. All the men in my life, they say, they think of me, as . . . as a *friend.* (*Pause*) A child deserves a father. A child deserves to know his or her father. But too bad, kiddo, life ain't fair, get used to it, you're stuck with me, and all the toys money can buy.

Look, I've looked at all the pros and cons, I've considered all the angles and the difficulties. I've thought about it and just because I don't have a man in my life . . . screw it. Being a mom is my dream. Being a parent, nourishing this little soul, giving guidance and direction and helping this little person be the best they can be. I want to experience the joys of childbirth. I've got a job that nets me six figures, CFO of a Fortune 500, I'm ready to slow down and be a good mom. (*She hears a knock at the door.*) Come on in, Doc. I'm ready!

Jim?

LAURA ZAM

DORA, a woman who has just turned 30, is talking to her husband who is reading a porno magazine.

DORA: Jim? Will you marry me? I know we're already married but if our marriage license was destroyed because of a storm in the Caribbean that came up the coast and then moved across America and our house just floated away, along with all of our important papers, and the license bureau didn't have a copy of the original because of wormy virus problems they tried for a whole year to fix but couldn't—they just couldn't prevent the loss of our marriage—would you marry me all over again? . . . Jim? . . . If you weren't reading right now, would you watch me? I mean would you look at me the way you're looking at the girls in that magazine? . . . Jim? I think I asked that wrong because what I really wanted to ask was if you like me better with my hair this way or the way I wore my hair last year. I had bangs. Remember the bangs? I just never had the chance to ask if you prefer me in bangs or not in bangs. . . . Jim? I really wish you'd stop looking at that magazine because I have some questions for you. Important, serious questions like whether or not you make love to other women when I visit my parents in Fort Lauderdale, or when I go get my back waxed, or when I have an all-day intensive on double chin prevention. Because I think you do. I'm beginning to think you do. . . . But maybe that's not important. . . . Maybe what I really should be asking is if you would ever punch me in the stomach or hold a serrated knife to my throat. That's what I really should be asking . . . Jim? Could you please stop reading and answer me because I really need to know some things? And I'm ready now. My birthday is tomorrow and I'm ready to hear about you, and I'm ready to hear about us . . .

Jim?!!!!! . . . OK, let's make a deal: If you stop reading, I'll stop asking questions . . . OK? SO CAN YOU PLEASE STOP LOOKING AT THAT MAGAZINE???? . . . Because I don't have any more questions in my throat, anyway. All I have is something else. I don't know what it is but it's not a question. I think it's an answer. An answer for us, Jim. I just decided: I want you to make me a baby. Jim. I want you to make me a baby. Jim. I want you to make me a baby. Jim? . . . Jim? . . . Jim? . . .

Contributors

Zakiyyah Alexander's work has been produced and/or developed at Greenwich Street Theatre (*Blurring Shrine*), New York International Fringe Festival, La MaMa E.T.C. (*Momentary Delay*), Pace Theatre (*After the Show*), and The Producer's Club (*One Smart Trick*). Her awards and fellowships include a Gilman fellowship at New Dramatists, a Drama League New Directors/New Works award, New Professional Theatre Prize, and a residency at New Perspectives Theatre. She is a current member of Ensemble Studio Theatre's Youngblood and of Women's Work Project Playwrights Lab, as well as being a resident playwright at New Dramatists. Having received her M.F.A. from the Yale School of Drama, she is the program director of a teen music company.

Rosanna Yamagiwa Alfaro is a playwright and short story writer. Her plays include *Behind Enemy Lines* (Pan Asian Repertory), *Mishima* (East West Players), *Martha Mitchell* (Edinburgh Fringe festival and Theatre Center, Philadelphia), *Matters of Life and Death* (Theatre Redux), *Barrancas* (Magic Theatre), *Pablo and Cleopatra* (New Theatre, Boston), *Mexico City* and *Sailing Down the Amazon* (Boston Women on Top Festival), and *It Doesn't Take a Tornado* and *Amsterdam* (La MaMa E.T.C.).

Janet Allard is a recipient of two Jerome Fellowships at The Playwrights' Center (2000–2001, 2002–2003). Her recent works include *Untold Crimes of Insomniacs*, which premiered at The Guthrie Lab in 2004, *Incognito* (Guthrie Theater commission), and *Loyal* (The Guthrie and The Children's Theatre Company in Minneapolis cocommission). *The Unknown: a silent musical* (a collaboration with director Jean Randich and composer Shane Rettig) was awarded a Jonathan Larson Fellowship and appeared in Joe's Pub as part of The Public

Theater's New Work Now Festival 2004. Allard's work has been seen at The Kennedy Center, Playwrights Horizons, Yale Rep, The Yale Cabaret, The Women's Project & Productions, The House of Candles, Access Theatre, and in Ireland, England, Greece, and New Zealand. She is a graduate of the Yale School of Drama.

Elizabeth Appleby is a performer and writer. Her one-woman show *Fritz Perls Is My (tor)Mentor* won the tenth anniversary competition at The Marsh in San Francisco where it was later produced. She is a recipient of a grant from the Zellerbach Family Fund.

Heidi Arneson is a writer, performer, and visual artist renowned for her one-woman shows about girlhood, sexuality, and American archetypes. Her plays include *Mary Margaret Please Appear, Degrade School, PreHansel and PostGretel, Homeland Security*, and *Ten Bedroom Heart*. Ms. Arneson is a recipient of the Bush Artist Fellowship and the Franklin Furnace Emerging Artist Award; she is a Core Alumna of The Playwrights' Center, and a 2005 Theater nominee for the prestigious Alpert Award in the Arts. She lives in Minneapolis, where she teaches weekly workshops on writing and performing.

Rachel Axler's plays have been produced by Vital Theatre Company, Spring Theatreworks, Cal Arts, and other companies in the New York and Los Angeles regions. Her work can be read at mcsweeneys.com and in various bathroom stalls across the United States. She received her B.A. from Williams College and her M.F.A. in playwriting from UCSD.

Anna Baum is a writer and director living in Los Angeles. Her plays have been read and produced in Boston, Cleveland, and Los Angeles. A published poet and journalist, she also wrote and coproduced the video *Out of Reach*. She recently received a grant from the Cambridge, Massachusetts Arts Council to write and produce a reading of *the persephone project*, a stage play based on the stories of survivors of domestic violence.

Monika Bustamante's plays have been performed in Austin, Chicago, Dallas, Houston, Los Angeles, Miami, New York, and abroad. *Set Up* is part one of the award-winning *Let Down/Raised Up Series*, a trilogy that premiered over three years at FronteraFest Short Fringe in Austin, Texas. Monika received an M.F.A. with a James Michener Fellowship in Playwriting from the University of Texas at Austin.

Sheila Callaghan's plays have been produced and developed with Soho Rep, Playwrights Horizons, South Coast Repertory, Clubbed Thumb, The LARK, Actors Theatre of Louisville, New Georges, Annex Theatre, Moving Arts, and LABrynth, among others. Sheila is the recipient of a Princess Grace award for emerging artists, an *LA Weekly* Award for Best One-Act, a Chesley Prize for Lesbian Playwriting, a MacDowell residency, a Jerome Fellowship, and an NYFA grant. Her plays include *Scab, The Hunger Waltz, Crawl Fade to White, Crumble (Lay Me Down, Justin Timberlake), We Are Not These Hands, Dead City, Lascivious Something, Kate Crackernuts,* and her opera, *Elemental* with music by Sophocles Papavasilopoulos. She teaches playwriting at The College of New Jersey and is a member of the playwrights' organization 13P.

Elena Carrillo is a writer, teacher, and producer living in Austin, Texas. For the past five years, she has been working with Austin ScriptWorks, a playwright's service organization, as a dramaturg and playwright. She is currently returning to her first love—prose—and writing a novel.

Katherine Catmull is an actor and writer in Austin, Texas. "Pizza Apostrophe" was first performed in a slightly longer version for the FronteraFest Short Fringe festival at the Hyde Park Theatre in January 2003. Katherine also contributed to the full-length play *Orange* produced in 2004 by Refraction Arts Project and nominated for the American Theatre Critics Association's annual ATCA/Steinberg New Play Award. Her freelance writing has appeared in *Salon*, *Stage Directions*, and the *Austin Chronicle*.

Vicki Caroline Cheatwood is a happy regional playwright, based in Dallas. Recent production highlights: *The Risen Chris* (Finalist, 2002 Heideman Award, Actors Theatre of Louisville), produced at Vital Theatre, New York; *The Cowgirl Chronicles*, produced by Actors Stock Company/NYC in Six Figures Theater Company's Artists of Tomorrow Series; *The Persistence of Memory*, produced by Seattle's Mae West Fest; *10:10*, produced by Ground Zero Theater Company, Dallas; and *The People*, "Best of Fest" pick in Atlantis Playmakers' Short Attention Span Playfest in Billerica, Massachusetts. Her unproduced full-length work *An Hour South* was a finalist for the Julie Harris Playwright Award.

Paula Cizmar's plays have been produced off-Broadway, in London, and from Maine to California. Among her honors are an NEA grant and a Rockefeller Foundation residency. Her plays include: *Street Stories*, *Candy and Shelley Go to the Desert*, and *Bone Dry*. She was a staff writer for the television series *American Family* for two seasons. She is a cofounder of New Powder Plays with Laura Shamas, with whom she wrote the performance piece *Venus in Orange*.

Véronique de Turenne is a journalist and screenwriter whose work has appeared in numerous newspapers and magazines including the *Los Angeles Times*, *Los Angeles Magazine*, the *Chicago Tribune*, *Miami Herald*, *Salon.com*, *Daily Variety*, *Wahine*, and *Simple Cooking*. Her essay about driving to the exact geographic center of California has been collected in *My California*. She lives in Malibu.

Lisa Dillman's plays have been produced at Steppenwolf, American Theatre Company, Transparent Theatre, and Hypothetical Theatre. Lisa has won a 2004 Sprenger-Lang New History Play Prize, the 2003 Sarett Award, first prize in the 1996 Midwestern Playwrights Festival, and a 1991 Julie Harris Award. She has received two commissions from Steppenwolf as well as fellowships from the Illinois Arts Council, the William Inge Foundation, and the O'Neill Playwrights Conference. Her work has been developed with the support of many groups including the Women's Project, Victory Gardens, Ensemble Studio Theatre, Famous Door, the Philadelphia Theatre Company and the Huntington Theatre Company.

Linda Eisenstein is a three-time recipient of Ohio Arts Council Individual Artist Playwriting Fellowships for *Three the Hard Way* and the musicals *Star Wares: The Next Generation* and *Discordia* (with James Levin). Other plays include *The Names of the Beast* (Sappho's Symposium Award) and *Marla's Devotion* (All-England Festival Prize). Her works have been produced throughout the United States and abroad. She is a member of the Cleveland Play House Playwrights' Unit.

Cynthia Franks' play *Hay* is a full-length work about our disappearing open land. Her other word includes: *The Lighthouse* (a semifinalist in the 2002 PlayLabs National Conference), *24 Etudes* (produced by Actors Studio, New York), *Then . . .* (produced by Cry Havoc Productions, New York), and *Art of the World Building* (produced by Studio Theatre, Detroit). Cynthia has been a playwright-in-residence at Visible Theatre, Inc., and writes for children's television. She has her M.F.A. from The Actors Studio Drama school, and her B.F.A. from Wayne State University. She is a member of the BMI Lehman Engle Musical Theatre Workshop, the Dramatists Guild, and the Writers Guild of America, East.

Melissa Gawlowski's play *An American Lamp* was staged at Ohio University in 2002. Her other works include *On the Line* and *The Critic*. Her play *The True Story of Harold Tubbsman* was selected for the 2002 American College Theatre Festival in Milwaukee. Her short play *Mimi Meets Her Match* was produced in New York by the 52nd Street Project. Her work was recently selected for an upcoming collection by Smith & Kraus.

Laurie Graff is a New York writer and actress whose credits include work on and off-Broadway, regionally, commercials, and print. A selection from her one-act play, *Charlie & Flo,* is published in *The Best Men's Stage Monologues 1999*. Her novel *You Have to Kiss a Lot of Frogs* (Red Dress Ink) will be followed by *Fear of Frogging* and *The Eight Dates of Hanukkah*, a chick-lit holiday anthology.

Ellen Hagan is a writer, performer, and educator. She holds an M.F.A. in fiction from The New School and has received grants from the Kentucky Foundation for Women. She has self-published several chapbooks and her work can be seen in the online journals *La Petite Zine* and *Failbetter*. She is currently working on her first novel, *The Kentucky Notes*.

Laura Harrington's award-winning plays and musicals have been produced regionally, off-Broadway, in Canada, and in Europe. Recent credits include: *Resurrection* (Houston Grand Opera), *The Book of Hours* (Wellesley Summer Theatre), *Hallowed Ground* (winner of the 2001 Boston "IRNE" Award for Best New Play), *Martin Guerre* (directed by Mark Lamos), *The Perfect 36, Joan of Arc*, and *Marathon Dancing* (directed by Anne Bogart). She is on the faculty at Harvard and M.I.T. and is the winner of a Massachusetts Cultural Council Playwriting Fellowship, and a two-time winner of the Clauder Playwriting Competition. Other awards include a Bunting Institute Fellowship, a Whiting Foundation Grant-in-Aid, and the Joseph Kesselring Award for Drama.

Tia Dionne Hodge is an award-nominated actress, writer, producer, and director. She received her M.A. and B.A. in English from Case Western Reserve University in 1996, and was the first recipient of the Louise Kent-Hope Award for Excellence in Poetry and Creative Writing from the Adrienne Kennedy Society. She is a former National Poetry Slam champion, and her essay, *Letter to Granma Gladys*, was published in the anthology *Black Comedy: 9 Plays*. Tia is a member of the New Jersey Dramatists & Waterfront Ensemble, the Dramatists Guild of America, SAG, AFTRA, and AEA.

Quiara Alegria Hudes' play *Yemaya's Belly* was produced by Portland Stage Company and Miracle Theatre Group. Her other plays include: *Holy Broth*, produced at Perishable Theatre and *The Adventures of Barrio Grrrl!*, produced at Miracle Theatre. Her work has been developed at South Coast Repertory, Manhattan Theatre Club, Page Seventy-Three Productions, the Kennedy Center, and Signature Theatre. She received a playwriting M.F.A. from Brown University.

Lindsay Brandon Hunter is an actor and playwright living in New York City, where she performs as a company member of the Neo-Futurists' *Too Much Light Makes the Baby Go Blind*. Her plays include *Licking Spalding Gray* (cowritten with Ben Laurance), *Like this*, and *Que Sera, My Darling*. Her work has been performed at On the Boards' 12 Minutes Max series, and at Seattle's Mae West Fest and 14/48 festivals.

Sandra Hunter's plays have been seen in London, New York, San Francisco, and Los Angeles. After the birth of her daughter, she began writing short stories, which have appeared or are forthcoming in the *Hawai'i Review*, *Glimmer Train*, *North Dakota Quarterly*, *Porcupine*, *Primavera*, and others.

Julie Jensen is the author of more than thirty plays. She is currently Resident Playwright at Salt Lake Acting Company where

"Water Lilies" premiered as a part of an evening of short plays in honor of the Olympics. She recently received a TCG/NEA Residency Grant and a major grant form the Pew Charitable Trusts. Her work is published by Dramatic Publishing.

Tania Katan is a graduate of the Arizona State University Theatre Program. Her awards include the American College Theatre Festival Award in Playwriting, the Jane Chambers Student Playwrights Award, and the A.C.T. David Mamet Playwriting Award. Her plays have been seen at many venues including Connecticut Repertory Theatre, Circle Repertory Theatre, A Traveling Jewish Theatre, and Pacific Resident Theatre. Tania's essays include "She Koogled Me," published in *Mentsh,* and "Mapping the Human Genome" in *Imagining Ourselves.* She regularly performs her essays at Comedy Central's Sit-n-Spin. Her memoir, *My One Night Stand with Cancer,* will be published in 2005 and her one-woman show based on the memoir will premier in 2005 at the Lily Tomlin/Jane Wagner Cultural Arts Center.

Elena Kaufman is from Vancouver, Canada, but lives in Paris. She holds an M.A. in Drama from the University of Toronto, and an Acting Diploma from The Academy Drama School in London. Her first produced play, *Miss/es,* was developed at FemFest in Winnipeg. She is presently corunning Paris Playwrights, an Anglophone playwrights lab, out of the Shakespeare & Company Bookstore in Paris. Upcoming is a reading of her full-length play, *MotherShip,* through Moving Parts, a bilingual playreading unit. She is also actively involved as an actress in the small but supportive Anglophone theatre community in Paris.

Sherry Kramer's work has been seen at theaters across America and abroad. She is a recipient of NEA, New York Foundation for the Arts, and McKnight Fellowships, the Weissberger Playwriting Award, a New York Drama League Award, and the

Marvin Taylor Award (for *What a Man Weighs*), the LA Women in Theater New Play Award (for *The Wall of Water*), and the Jane Chambers Playwriting Award (for *David's RedHaired Death*). The first national member of New Dramatists, she teaches playwriting at the Michener Center for Writers at the University of Texas, Austin, and at the Iowa Playwrights Workshop. Her plays are published by Broadway Publishing. "The God of This" is excerpted from *The Mad Master.*

Carson Kreitzer's plays include *The Love Song of J. Robert Oppenheimer, Slither, Self Defense or death of some salesmen, The Slow Drag,* and *Take My Breath Away,* and have been produced in New York, Los Angeles, Chicago, Cincinnati, Minneapolis, Providence, and London. She is a member of the Dramatists Guild and The Playwrights' Center, and has received grants from NYFA, NYSCA, the NEA, TCG, and the Jerome and McKnight Foundations. She currently lives in Austin, Texas.

Diane Lefer is a playwright, award-winning fiction writer, artistic associate of Playwrights' Arena (which will produce her play *Harvest* as part of the 2005 season), and contributing writer to *LA Stage* magazine. The full-length play *Penalty Phase* had a staged reading by Indie Chi Productions at the McCadden Place Theatre in Los Angeles en route to an expected production. The excerpted monologue was first performed by Amy Hill for Hot Night in the City, the Playwrights' Arena benefit at the Los Angeles Theater Center. Her books include *The Circles I Move In, Radiant Hunger,* and *Very Much Like Desire.*

Barbara (Babs) Lindsay is a fifth generation Californian living very happily in Seattle. Her numerous plays have had more than 65 national and international productions. More than one hundred of her original monologues can be found at www.themonologueshop.com. She feels her most important work to date has been to compose the Activist's Credo: *Do what you can. Begin at home.*

Jennifer Maisel's plays, including *Mallbaby*, *Eden*, *Dark Hours*, *Mad Love*, and . . . *And The Two Romeos*, have been work-shopped and produced in Chicago, New York, Minneapolis, San Francisco, and Los Angeles, as well as regionally. She received both the Charlotte Woolard award for most promising new writer and the Fund for New American Plays award from the Kennedy Center for *The Last Seder*, which premiered at Chicago's Organic Theatre and was then produced at Theatre J in Washington, DC.

Elizabeth Dañiel Marquis was born and raised in Cypress, Texas. She received her B.F.A. in Dramatic Writing from NYU's Tisch School of the Arts, where she won the Rod Marriott Senior Playwriting Award. Her plays have been produced in New York, San Francisco, and Austin. A violinist and poet as well, she lives with her sister Francesca, a muralist, shadow pup-peteer, and cake decorator. Together, they are know as the Seriously Silly Sisters Shadow Puppetry Troupe. At the moment, she is an English teacher and has been living and working in Italy for the past year.

Ellen McLaughlin's productions include *The Persians* (National Actors' Theater), *A Narrow Bed* (New York Theater Workshop and Actors Theatre of Louisville), *Tongue of a Bird* and *Helen* (The Public Theater), *Iphigenia and Other Daughters* (Classic Stage Company, New York), and *Days and Nights Within* and *Infinity's House* (both at Actors Theatre of Louisville). Other producing venues include The Mark Taper Forum, The Intiman Theater, Oregon Shakespeare Festival, and The Almeida Theater in London. She has received NEA awards, the Susan Smith Blackburn Prize, and awards from the Lila Wallace–Reader's Digest Fund.

Brighde Mullins' plays have been performed in London, New York, and San Francisco. Her titles include *Those Who Can, Do*; *Monkey in the Middle*; *Topographical Eden*; and *Fire Eater*. Her book of poems is *Water Stories.* She has received a Whiting Award and an NEA Fellowship. She teaches at Harvard University.

Lizzie Olesker's plays include *Verdure, Dreaming through History, Razing Houses, Ruby's Shoe, Gowanus Girl,* and *Alcestis* (an adaptation, commissioned by the Public Theater). Her work has been presented at The Cherry Lane Theatre (with the Mentor Project), New Georges/HERE, and 78th Street Theater/Sightlines Theater Co. She has been a performer and collaborator with the Talking Band and Paradise Opera, and has received fellowships from NYFA and the Dramatists Guild. She teaches playwriting at New York University and Swarthmore College and lives in Brooklyn with her husband (a professional stuntman) and their three children. She is a member of the Brooklyn Writers Space.

Jamie Pachino's plays *Splitting Infinity, Waving Goodbye, The Return to Morality, Aurora's Motive,* and *Race* have won over a dozen awards including the Kennedy Center Fund for New American Plays and Chicago's Joseph Jefferson ("Jeff") Award for Best New Work. Her work has been seen in four countries, commissioned, published, and optioned for the screen. She is currently at work on a new play commission for Steppenwolf Theatre, a blind script deal with DreamWorks, and screenplays for LifeTime Television and Vanguard Films.

Talia Pura is a writer and actor, currently living near Winnipeg, Manitoba, where she teaches drama at the University of Winnipeg. Many of her plays have been performed, including independent productions in Winnipeg, Toronto, Minneapolis, and New York City. Her works include *Delivery* (a short drama, published in the anthology *Instant Applause II*), *Hillary* (a radio drama commissioned by the C.B.C. (Canadian public radio), and *Stages: Creative Ideas for Teaching Drama* (a book published by J. Gordon Shillingford Publishing, Inc.).

Erin M. Pushman is a Michigan-born playwright living and working in the Carolinas. She draws often on her family roots, which extend from the Appalachian mountains to the Detroit steel mills, to create her plays. Her award-winning full-length, one-act, and short plays have been produced in Iowa City, Charlotte, and Raleigh, North Carolina, and her poems and creative nonfiction essays have appeared in several journals. Currently she is an English professor at Limestone College.

Nina Rapi's recent plays include *Edgewise* (Gate Theatre with TheatreLab script-in-hand performance), *Lovers* (Gielgud Theatre, West End Shorts season), *Josie's Restrooms* (ICA, monologue published by Robinson), *Angelstate* (awarded an Arts Council Writing Bursary and a London Writers prize for its extract *Confession*), *Tricky* (Tart Gallery, monologue). Earlier work includes: *Dance of Guns & Dreamhouses* (both at Oval House Theatre), *Ithaka* (Riverside Studios staged reading, published by Aurora Metro in *Seven Plays by Women*, winner of the Raymond Williams award), and *Critical Moments* (Soho Poly Theatre, a trilogy of shorts). Her nonfiction and short stories have been published in the UK, United States, Italy, and Greece.

Jacquelyn Reingold's plays, which include *String Fever, Girl Gone, Dear Kenneth Blake, Tunnel of Love, Freeze Tag, Acapulco*, and *For-everett*, have been seen in New York at Ensemble Studio Theatre, MCC, Naked Angels, and HB Playwrights. She has been the recipient of the New Dramatists' Whitfield Cook and Joe Callaway awards, two Drama-Logues, as well as funding through an EST/Sloan Commission and the Kennedy Center's Fund for New American Plays. She received her M.F.A. in playwriting in 2004 from Ohio University.

Molly Rice is a recipient of the Lucille Lortel Fellowship in Playwriting at Brown University, where she is presently an M.F.A. candidate. A native Texan, her plays have been developed, published, and produced in New York City, Austin,

Dallas, and Providence. Having spent time as a rock musician, a fry cook, a professional trainer, a cancer information specialist, and a hotel lounge promoter, she is pleased to now be focused solely on playwriting.

Tania Richard's plays include *Happy. Go. Lucky.* (winner, Firehouse Theatre Project's Festival of New Plays and finalist, Seanachi Theatre's Amarach Play Festival), *Selecting Memory* (winner, Seanachi Theatre's Amarach Play Festival), *Variations on a Theme* (finalist, Famous Doors—Women at the Door), *Tru Imagined Life* (Equity Library Theatre's Outreach), *Bitty Danvers' Family Stump, An Evening with Renee Lawrence,* and *Internally Yours.* She was commissioned by Healthworks Theatre to write an original script on HIV prevention. She holds a B.S. in theatre from Illinois State University.

Robin Rothstein's plays and monologues include, among others, *Clue Phone* (published in *Even More Monologues for Women by Women*), *In a Manner of Speaking* (Actors Theatre of Louisville premiere, Heideman Award finalist, published in *2004 The Best Ten-Minute Plays 2 Actors*), and her award-winning off-Broadway play, *On Deaf Ears.* Her plays have also been finalists for the Jane Chambers Playwriting Award and the Kernodle New Play Competition. Robin dedicates "True" to Dr. Daniel Roses, Dr. Mihye Choi, Dr. Judith Kaufer, Robin Kleinman, Bette Jan Rosenhagen, Judith Hirsch, and Sunsh Stein.

Louise Rozett has had the good fortune to see her work produced by great companies such as Chicago Dramatists Workshop and Naked Angels. She holds a B.A. in psychology from Vassar College and an M.F.A. in acting from The Theatre School at DePaul University. Her latest play, *Break*, was workshopped at New York Stage & Film in 2004, starring Tony Award–winner Frank Wood.

Sarah Ruhl's plays include *The Clean House* (Susan Smith Blackburn Award), *Melancholy Play, Eurydice, Late: a cowboy song, Orlando,* and *Passion Play.* Her plays have been produced around the country and in London and Germany. She received her M.F.A. from Brown University, and is originally from Chicago. In 2003, she was the recipient of a Helen Merrill award and a Whiting Writers' award. She is a member of New Dramatists.

Kristan Ryan is a Southern playwright and novelist living in New York City. Her one-act play *How Lorelei Lovejay Became a Love Goddess and Queen of the Dyke-O-Rama* was produced by the Philadelphia Gay and Lesbian Theatre Festival, her play *The Widowmaker* was translated into French (*Le Fraiseur de Veuves*) and produced by the Theatre du Centaure of Luxembourg, and her monologue *How Miss Brenda Lou Turpin Became Miss Save the Babies and a Star for Jesus* was performed at FirstStage Theatre, Los Angeles. Kristan teaches drama, English composition, American literature, and other writing-related courses at Interboro Institute in New York City.

Francesca Sanders is an award-winning playwright whose work has graced stages from New York to Alaska. She began her writing career in January, 2000 quite by accident—literally (broken elbow)—and since then has completed fourteen full-length plays including *Rising from the Sugar Bowl, To Wait in Heavy Harness, The Rustling Wheat,* and *I Become a Guitar,* to name a few.

Lisa Schlesinger's stage and radio plays include *The Bones of Danny Winston, Manny and Chicken, Bow Echo, Rock Ends Ahead,* and *Celestial Bodies.* Her work has been commissioned, produced, and broadcast in the United States, Europe, and Africa. She has received awards from the NEA, CEC International, and the BBC. She lives with musician Ben Schmidt and their children in Iowa City.

Laura Shamas, Ph.D., has written twenty-four plays, a playwriting textbook, and a rock and roll book. Some of her published plays include: *Lady-Like, Portrait of a Nude, Picnic at Hanging Rock* (adaptation), *Amelia Lives,* and *The Other Shakespeare.* Her playwriting awards include The Warner Brothers Award, a Drama-Logue Award, and an Edinburgh Fringe First Award for Outstanding New Drama. Recent productions include *Re-Sourcing,* produced at the NoHo Arts Center, Los Angeles, in 2004 and the cowritten collage play *Venus in Orange* (with Paula Cizmar), to be produced in Los Angeles in 2005.

S. M. Shephard-Massat attended New York University's Tisch School for the Arts and spent a year in London interning at the Royal Court Theatre. Her plays include: *Waiting to be Invited* (which won the Young Dramatist's Award from the Adrienne Kennedy Society, a Roger L. Stevens grant, the Westword Best of Denver 2000 Award for Best New Play, and the Osborn Award given by the American Theatre Critics Association for 2001), *Someplace Soft to Fall* (produced by the Penumbra Theatre Company, St. Paul, Minnesota, and recipient of the Francesca Primus Award), and *Levee James* (produced at the O'Neill Playwrights Conference and A.C.T in San Francisco, also recipient of the BTAA Award for best playwriting, 2002).

Lydia Stryk is the author of ten full-length plays including *Safe House, Lady Lay, The Glamour House, The House of Lily,* and most recently, *On Clarion* and *American Tet.* Her plays have been produced at Steppenwolf, Victory Gardens, Denver Center Theater, Perseverance Theatre, and Schauspiel Essen as well as Theaterhaus Stuttgart in Germany, among others, and seen at festivals and in readings around the country and off-Broadway. She is a recipient of a Berrilla Kerr Foundation Playwright's Award.

Shanessa Sweeney studies graduate acting at Brandeis University. Originally from Dayton, Ohio, she was the first in her immediate family to go away to college. She has been performing in several capacities since she came into the world. Being selected to attend The Young Authors Conference was the first in a string of writing, speech, acting, and dancing accomplishments. She is a poet and spoken word performer and created *Poetically Correct*, an annual showcase for talented poets and writers from the Alabama State University campus (where she was an undergraduate) and surrounding community.

Freyda Thomas has been an actor, playwright, college instructor, high school French teacher, big band vocalist, cruiseship chanteuse, banjo bandleader, realtor, office manager, dog walker and nanny. She holds an M.F.A. in playwriting from CalArts. Her plays include *The Gamester* (Northlight Theatre, Repertory Theatre of St. Louis, and A.C.T San Francisco), *The Heir Transparent* (Alabama Shakespeare Festival, The Will Geer Theatricum Botanicum, Florida Studio Theatre), and translations of *The Learned Ladies* and *Tartuffe* (*Tartuffe: Born Again*), both published by Samuel French. *The Gamester* (based on *Le Joueur* by Jean-Francois Regnard) is slated for publication in the spring of 2005. She recently completed *School for Trophy Wives*, a new Molière adaptation.

Alice Tuan is the author of *Last of the Suns, Ikebana, Some Asians, Ajax (por nobody), Coastline, Iggy Woo,* and *Hit*. Adaptations include *The Roaring Girle* and *Ah Q*. Short works include *Cricket* (from *The Square*), *That Race Place* (from *Cootie Shots*), *Coco Puffs, F.E.T.C.H.,* and *The Hairy Tenor*. Essays include "The Crisis of Label" and "Virtual Hypertext Theater: A Luddite's Foray into Technology." She holds an M.F.A. from Brown University.

Kathryn Walat's plays include *Rotten State* (Bay Area Playwrights Festival), *Know Dog* (Salvage Vanguard, Hangar Theatre), *Johnny Hong Kong* (Perishable Theatre/Women's Playwriting Festival), and *A Book of Two* (Yale Drama School

Thesis). She currently lives in New York, where her work has appeared at Ensemble Studio Theatre, New Dramatists, and New Georges, where she is an affiliated playwright. She received her B.A. from Brown University, and her M.F.A. from Yale Drama School.

Barbara Wiechmann is a New York-based playwright and performer whose plays have been produced in New York, Chicago, Seattle, Philadelphia, and many other places around the country. Her play *Feeding the Moonfish* is including in *Telling Tales*, a collection of short plays. She is a member of New Dramatists and a graduate of Hamilton College.

Elizabeth Wong's plays include *The Love Life of a Eunuch*, *Dating and Mating in Modern Times* (from which "Love Juice" is excerpted), *China Doll*, *Letters to a Student Revolutionary*, and *Kimchee & Chitlins*. The Kennedy Center commissioned her to write the libretto for her adaptation of Oscar Wilde's *The Happy Prince*. Her television credits include: the ABC sitcom *All-American Girl*, and the Disney Writing Fellowship. She is affiliated with PEN, the Dramatists Guild, ASSITEJ, and WGAwest. She holds an M.F.A. from NYU's Tisch School of the Arts and she teaches playwriting at the University of California, Santa Barbara.

Laura Zam is a writer and a performer. In New York, her theatrical work has been presented at The Public Theater, Ensemble Studio Theatre, and others. In Europe, her one-woman play *Circles, Holes, and Arches* played for a year in Prague. Awards include: the Amiri Baraka Literary Prize, an Open Society Fund grant, a Tennessee Williams Fellowship, and a Salomon grant. She has taught at the University of California, Berkeley and at Brown University, where she received her M.F.A. in Creative Writing.

Performance Rights

For Zakiyyah Alexander, contact the author at *zrahiim@hotmail.com*.

For Rosanna Yamagiwa Alfaro, contact the author at *alfaros@comcast.net*.

For Janet Allard, contact the author through The Playwrights Center, 2301 Franklin Ave. E., Minneapolis, MN 55406; 612-332-7481; *www.pwcenter.org*. Some scripts available through Playscripts, Inc., P.O. Box 237060, New York, NY 10023; 866-639-7529; *www.playscripts.com*.

For Elizabeth Appleby, contact Heinemann.

For Heidi Arneson, contact the author at *Heidihouse1@yahoo.com*.

For Rachel Axler, contact the author at *rachel_axler@ yahoo.com.*

For Anna Baum, contact the author at *ambaum@earthlink.net.*

For Monika Bustamante, contact the author at *ukmonika@yahoo.com.*

For Sheila Callaghan, contact the author at s*heila_callaghan@ hotmail.com.*

For Elena Carrillo, contact the author at *your_quagga@yahoo.com.*

For Katherine Catmull, contact the author at *kathy@ hydeparktheatre.org.*

For Vicki Caroline Cheatwood, contact the author at *vcc2112@ earthlink.net.*

For Paula Cizmar, contact the author at *pcizmar@earthlink.net.*

For Véronique de Turenne, contact the author at *turenne@ earthlink.net.*

For Lisa Dillman, contact Selma Lultinger at Robert A. Freedman Dramatic Agency, 1501 Broadway, Suite 2310, New York, NY 10036; ph: 212-840-5760; fax: 212-840-5776.

For Linda Eisenstein, contact the author through Herone Press, 1378 W. 64th Street, Cleveland, OH 44102; 216-961-5624; *plays@lindaeisenstein.com.*

For Cynthia Franks, contact the author at *cynfrank@aol.com.*

For Melissa Gawlowski, contact the author at *mgawlowski@ hotmail.com.*

For Laurie Graff, contact Robert Youdelman, Attorney, 19 West 44th Street, New York, NY 10036; ph: 212-575-8500.

For Ellen Hagan, contact Heinemann.

For Laura Harrington, contact the author at *harringt@gis.net.*

For Tia Dionne Hodge, contact the author at *tiadhodge@ comcast.net.*

For Quiara Alegría Hudes, contact the author at *quiara@ quiara.com*.

For Lindsay Brandon Hunter, contact the author at *lindsaybrandon@hotmail.com*.

For Sandra Hunter, contact the author at *tinyhuntress@ earthlink.net*.

For Julie Jenson, contact the author at Salt Lake Acting Company, 168 West 500 North, Salt Lake City, UT 84103; ph: 801-596-2941; fax: 801-532-8513; *julietwoheaded@ aol.com*.

For Tania Katan, contact the author at *herpulserunsriot@ hotmail.com*.

For Elena Kaufman, contact the author at *elenaloo@yahoo.com*.

For Sherry Kramer, contact the author at *SherryLKramer@ aol.com*.

For Carson Kreitzer, contact the author at *cskreitzer@ earthlink.net*.

For Diane Lefer, contact the author at *desilef@cs.com*.

For Barbara Lindsay, contact the author at *babzella@ earthlink.net*.

For Jennifer Maisel, contact Susan Schulman Literary Agency, 454 W. 44th Street, New York, NY 10036; ph: 212-713-1633; fax: 212-581-8830; *schulman@aol.com*.

For Elizabeth Dañiel Marquis, contact the author at *eruptingvolcano@juno.com*.

For Ellen McLaughlin, contact Joyce Ketay, The Joyce Ketay Agency, 630 Ninth Ave., Suite 706, New York, NY 10036; 212-354-6825; *joyce@joyceketay.com*.

For Brighde Mullins, contact Charles Kopelman, 393 W. 49th St. Suite 5G, New York, NY 10019; ph: 212-445-0160; fax: 212-246-7138; *ckopelman@dandkartists.com*.

For Lizzie Olesker, contact the author at *lizzieo@ mindspring.com*.

For Jamie Pachino, contact the author through Writers & Artists, 19 W. 44th Street, Suite 1000, New York, NY; ph: 212-391-1112; fax: 212-575-6397.

For Talia Pura, contact the author at *tpura@mts.net.*

For Erin M. Pushman, contact the author at *pushmane@aol.com.*

For Nina Rapi, contact the author at *ninarapi@aol.com.*

For Jacquelyn Reingold, contact Scott Yoselow, The Gersh Agency, 41 Madison Ave., 33rd Fl, New York, NY 10010; ph: 212-634-8102; fax: 212-391-8459; *syoselow@gershny.com.*

For Molly Rice, contact the author at *molly@commoner.com.*

For Tania Richard, contact the author at *taniajr@webtv.net.*

For Robin Rothstein, contact Ronald Gwiazida, Agent, Rosenstone-Wender, 38 East 29th St., 10th Fl, New York, NY 10016; ph: 212-725-9445; fax: 212-725-9447; *rosenstone@ aol.com.*

For Louise Rozett, contact the author at *scoobyroz@aol.com.*

For Sarah Ruhl, contact Bruce Ostler, Bret Adams, Ltd., 448 W. 44th Street, New York, NY 10036; ph: 212-765-5640; fax: 212-265-2212; *bostler.bal@verizon.net.*

For Kristan Ryan, contact *cmyagent@aol.com.*

For Francesca Sanders, contact the author at *arpius@ peoplepc.com.*

For Lisa Schlesinger, contact The Rod Hall Agency Ltd., 7 Goodge Place, London, England W1T 1FL; ph: (44) 171-637-0706; fax: (44) 171-637-0807; *charlotte@ rodhallagency.org.*

For Laura Shamas, contact Beth Blickers, Abrams Artists Agency, 275 Seventh Ave. 26th Floor, New York, NY 10001; ph: 646-486-4600; fax: 646-486-2363; *b.blickers@abramsart.com.*

For S. M. Shephard-Massat, contact Bruce Ostler, Bret Adams, Ltd., 448 W. 44th Street, New York, NY 10036; ph: 212-765-5640; fax: 212-265-2212; *bostler.bal@verizon.net*.

For Lydia Stryk, contact Mary Harden, Agent, Harden-Curtis Associates, 850 7th Ave., Suite 903, New York, NY 10036; ph: 212-977-8502; fax: 212-977-8420; *maryharden@hardencurtis.com*.

For Shanessa Sweeney, contact Sharon Gilmore at 2312 Davue Cir. #3, Dayton, OH 45406; ph: 937-274-1601; *sgilmore@dps.k12.oh.us*.

For Freyda Thomas, contact the author at *freydaz@yahoo.com*.

For Alice Tuan, contact Joyce Ketay, The Joyce Ketay Agency, 630 Ninth Ave., Suite 706, New York, NY 10036; 212-354-6825; *joyce@joyceketay.com*.

For Kathryn Walat, contact the author at *kathrynwalat@yahoo.com*.

For Barbara Wiechmann, contact New Dramatists, 424 W. 44th Street, New York, NY 10036; ph: 212-757-6960; fax: 212-265-4738; *newdramatists@newdramastists.org*.

For Elizabeth Wong, contact the author at *Elizabeth@elizabethwong.net*.

For Laura Zam, contact the author at *Laurazam@earthlink.net*.